LUDWIG VAN BEETHOVEN

AUTOGRAPH MISCELLANY FROM *CIRCA* 1786 TO 1799

BRITISH MUSEUM ADDITIONAL MANUSCRIPT 29801, ff. 39–162

(THE 'KAFKA SKETCHBOOK')

VOLUME II · TRANSCRIPTION

EDITED BY JOSEPH KERMAN

PROFESSOR OF MUSIC, UNIVERSITY OF CALIFORNIA AT BERKELEY

LONDON 1970

PUBLISHED BY THE TRUSTEES OF THE BRITISH MUSEUM

WITH THE CO-OPERATION OF THE ROYAL MUSICAL ASSOCIATION

SET NUMBER SBN 7141 0465 5
VOLUME I   SBN 7141 0466 3
VOLUME II   SBN 7141 0467 1

0714104655

PRINTED IN GREAT BRITAIN
AT THE UNIVERSITY PRESS, OXFORD
BY VIVIAN RIDLER
PRINTER TO THE UNIVERSITY

CONTENTS

AUTOGRAPH MISCELLANY FROM *CIRCA* 1786 TO 1799

INTRODUCTION

THE Beethoven autograph manuscript here published in facsimile and transcription consists of miscellaneous sheets and bifolia, a total of 124 folios dating from around 1786 to 1799. Beethoven used these sheets for autograph copies of works that he had completed or meant to complete, sketches and drafts of known and unknown compositions, and for many other notations of various sorts. A survey of the contents of the miscellany has been provided in the introduction to Volume I, which also includes material about the history and the physical characteristics of the manuscript. It remains for the introduction to Volume II to deal, broadly, with matters of interpretation, and in particular to discuss the procedures that have been adopted for the transcription.

The best course will be to begin with a concise statement of the editorial procedures; these have to be understood before the transcription volume can be put to use. The point of the procedures will emerge more clearly from the discussion of the problems of reading and interpreting Beethoven's sketches which follows later in the introduction.

★　　　★　　　★

The transcription presented here is not of the so-called 'diplomatic' type, which follows the original notation as faithfully as possible, adding nothing, correcting nothing, and reproducing the distribution and spacing of the music page by page and line by line. An attempt has been made to achieve a greater degree of intelligibility in the end result. Thus in the actual process of transcription, additions and emendations are made systematically in the many places where the manuscript

reading is incomplete or ambiguous, in order to normalize the notation and facilitate reading. The customary typographical devices are employed to distinguish editorial additions from material that appears in the source. Square brackets enclose editorial clefs, signatures, song texts, etc.; dotted lines are used for editorial barlines and ties; rests and accidentals added by the editor are printed in small music type. In cases of emendation, the original readings are shown *in situ*—original rhythms by means of indications such as 'ms: ♫', original pitches by means of italicized letters (*e, f*) next to the emended notes. (Letters in bold type such as **e, f, fis,** however, are Beethoven's own.) Questionable readings are pointed out by question marks.

The spacing of the notes and the direction of their stems, two features which are highly irregular in Beethoven's script, have both been normalized without special comment. On the other hand, in piano scores the distribution of notes between the two staffs has not been changed, even when this is peculiar. Nor has it seemed necessary to spell out Beethoven's various abbreviation symbols—'bis', '8va', ♃, //, and the like. When in a piano score one staff is entirely blank, it has been omitted from the transcription.

The individual sketches and other items, which are often run together and otherwise confused in the manuscript, have been separated from one another. A reference to folio, line, and bar (e.g. $\frac{116^v}{8/2}$) precedes each new item; these numerical references serve not only to locate the various items but also to distinguish and isolate them. Many sketches also receive brief descriptive titles (in square brackets). When the point of beginning or end of a sketch is in question, this is indicated.

Beethoven frequently cancelled notes and passages or otherwise altered them. In such cases the original reading has been indicated (whenever it can be read) in small music type or ordinary music type with cancellation lines through it. A mark (⸨⸩) has been devised for illegible cancellations. At times these procedures merely highlight slips of the pen, of course, but at other times they record part of the compositional process, something which is likely to be at the centre of interest for those using the present publication. The same procedures are followed with the autograph copies, once again with a view to the likely use of this edition. The reader will understand that these scores, as fully set forth here with variants, cancellations, and corrections, are not usable as critical editions, much less as performing editions. There would seem to be little point in duplicating scores that are for the most part available elsewhere.

In the matter of the arrangement of material, this edition follows two different principles, depending on the nature of the material transcribed. In part 1 of the transcription, sketches have been extracted from the miscellaneous folios and grouped under the works to which they refer. And under each individual composition or movement, sketches are placed in an order that will, it is hoped, make the compositional process as clear as the existing material permits. Sometimes this is the order of the manuscript, sometimes a putative chronological order; sometimes sketches are distributed according to the section of the work to which they refer (e.g. first theme, bridge, coda, etc.). When there are many sketches for a certain movement, it seems clearest to group them according to successive 'phases' of composition (see Op. 14, Op. 19, and the unfinished Sonata Movement in C minor and Symphony in C). An effort has been

x

made to follow Beethoven's own cross-reference system of 'Vide' and other signs and present the indicated sequence of ideas consecutively. Furthermore, shorter variant passages and rewritings have been aligned spatially with the main sketches and drafts. In general the arrangement has been designed to facilitate study of the sketches.

In part 1, where the sketches are grouped under the works sketched, the works themselves are arranged in three series. These are works with opus number, ordered numerically; works without opus number, ordered numerically by the 'WoO' (*Werke ohne Opuszahl*) numbers assigned in the Kinsky–Halm Catalogue; and other works—unfinished, uncatalogued, hitherto unknown, or lost—arranged alphabetically by title. The unfinished works in the last series are restricted to those that are copied or sketched fairly extensively, enough to allow a more or less coherent idea to be formed of their nature, at least as this was taking shape in Beethoven's mind. In practice this means that for sonata movements, and so on, about a page of sketches in transcription has to be present at the minimum. For songs and canons, less may suffice.

Isolating the unfinished works has involved some conjecture on the part of the editor, as has also the assignment of titles to them, for the genre is seldom identified in the manuscript or known from other sources. However, identifications can generally be made with a fair degree of certainty, and each case is discussed in the notes. Transcriptions of the autographs are also included in part 1, in their appropriate numerical or alphabetical order.

In addition to autographs, sketches for known works, and sketches for unknown works that show some coherence, the miscellany also includes many less coherent sketches, some studies, exercises, copies of other composers' music, and a mass of miscellaneous notations. To classify these would be of questionable value, and part 2 of the transcription volume simply presents them in the sequence of the manuscript, folio by folio. At the entry for each folio in part 2, cross-references are provided to autographs and sketches that have been extracted from it for inclusion in part 1.

Therefore when the reader wishes to consult the autograph or sketches for a particular work, he should refer to the appropriate place in part 1 of the transcription. When he has the facsimile open before him and wishes to see the transcription of a particular passage, he should turn directly to part 2. Under the folio in question he will see the passage transcribed, or else he will see a cross-reference to the page in part 1 where the transcription will be found.

*   *   *

The editorial procedures outlined above require some further discussion, for they differ in a number of respects from those employed in other well-known publications of Beethoven sketches. Certain differences may be accounted for by the character of the London miscellany itself, others by some legitimate variation in the interpretation of the aims and canons of scholarly editing. It will probably be widely agreed that the prime aim of an edition is to make material available, and that the further aim of a scholarly edition is to present the material as correctly and objectively as may be, in a form that makes the relation of the edition to the original source entirely clear. Beyond this point, however, differences of emphasis will appear. The degree of availability to be sought in an edition obviously depends on the sort of readers who are envisaged, and the level of objectivity that can be obtained varies considerably from situation to situation. Editors of Beethoven sketches,

facing problems in both areas that are in some ways especially severe, have arrived at different solutions.

The first and still the most famous of these scholars, Gustav Nottebohm, probably never entertained the possibility of a complete sketchbook transcription. In his best-known work, the monograph on the 'Eroica' sketchbook, 1880, Nottebohm did not attempt to present the entire source or even a good fraction of it, and gave scanty information about the context of the individual sketches and drafts. These he silently emended, brought into more or less conventional notation, abbreviated at will, and rearranged in an order designed to elucidate the compositional process. The attitude of modern Beethoven scholars towards such informal practices can well be imagined; yet in the wider sphere, Nottebohm's work on the sketches has been and continues to be by far the most influential. His editions are reprinted (most recently in 1970) and read widely, as such things go, up to the present day. The most significant modern work on the sketches is contained in the complete sketchbook edition begun in 1952 by the Beethovenhaus at Bonn. This employs the 'diplomatic' method whereby sketchbooks are transcribed completely, page by page, line by line, and even inch by inch— for an effort is made in the music-press to simulate the spacing of the original source. No concessions beyond the use of music type are made to easy reading or interpretation, so that the reader must on his own supply clefs and accidentals, fill in suspected omissions, attempt to unscramble and isolate the sketches— which are often very thoroughly confused indeed on the page— and draw his own conclusions as to their relationship to other sketches. In short, these transcriptions are half-facsimiles, too coarse as facsimiles for scholarly purposes yet faithful enough to transmit many of the main enigmas found in the original source. Except among a very small group of specialists, this edition has, predictably, made little impact. The same must be said for the prototype edition which pioneered the 'diplomatic' method of transcription, a sketchbook of 1800 published in 1927 by Lothar Mikulicz.[1]

The results achieved by both Nottebohm and the Beethovenhaus editors within their appointed limits are extremely impressive; but the limits themselves have not gone unquestioned.[2] Experience with these publications has persuaded many interested students that with Beethoven sketches desiderata of objectivity and availability cannot really be met by publication in a single version. A double version is necessary: a true facsimile, to meet the first of these desiderata, plus a carefully edited transcription to go some way towards meeting the second. A precedent for this admittedly somewhat luxurious solution has been provided by the recent edition of a sketchbook of 1802–3 in the Glinka Museum, Moscow, by N. L. Fishman, and by an older Bonn publication, a small edition of several sketch pages in the Beethovenhaus collection, by Arnold Schmitz (*Beethoven : Unbekannte Skizzen und Entwürfe*, 1924). In terms of editorial method, Schmitz's volume has proved to be the most suggestive model for the present publication, the more so since the material treated closely resembles that of the London miscellany.

The editing of sketches can of course never be accomplished with the objectivity expected in the more usual editorial process involving completed works. With completed works, it is to be assumed that the author had something definite in mind which he attempted to express clearly; errors and ambiguities may have entered in, but the editor can hope to identify these, emend or resolve them, and determine the author's intention with a fair degree of objectivity. With sketches, on the other hand, the author is under no constraint to express himself clearly, especi-

xii

ally since much of the time his intention is not clear to himself; and this is to say nothing of handwriting that may be, and in Beethoven's case notably is, hasty and imprecise. 'Ambiguity', 'error', 'emendation'—these are tricky concepts when applied to sketches. In an edition of Beethoven sketches, then, a considerable amount of interpretation is unavoidable, not only in the transcription proper—the reading of individual notes and passages—but also as regards numerous questions that may be described as questions of context. Even when the readings themselves are certain, it may not be certain where one sketch ends and a new one begins, whether a sketch is fully continuous or covers tacit breaks in sequence, in what order sketches were written, how they are related to other sketches in the vicinity or elsewhere, and so on.

In a situation of this sort there is a clear need for a facsimile. A facsimile allows, indeed encourages, the reader to check every reading. Of those readings marked by the editor as conjectural but probable, the degree of probability can be gauged. Also in the important matter of interpreting context, the facsimile makes available all the evidence, or at least as much of it as photographic means allow.

The editor of a sketchbook who is restricted to a single version, i.e. a transcription, will feel a strong obligation towards the original source. Knowing that its interpretation is frequently conjectural, he may well wish to make the transcription mirror the source, even if the edition that results may admittedly be

[1] The first even moderately extended discussion of this sketchbook appeared in Kurt Westphal, *Vom Einfall zur Symphonie*, Berlin, 1965. The three volumes that have been issued since 1952 in the Beethovenhaus sketchbook edition have yet to receive analytical treatment at any length. For a brief effort along these lines, see Joseph Kerman, 'Beethoven Sketchbooks in the British Museum', *Proceedings of the Royal Musical Association*, cxiii (1967), 85–94.

[2] Nottebohm's work has been often criticized. On the 'diplomatic' method of transcription, see Lewis Lockwood in *Musical Quarterly*, liii (1967), 128–36.

very hard to use. However, when the material is presented in a double version conditions are changed appreciably. The facsimile, desirable first of all on grounds of scholarly objectivity, also permits more latitude in the design of methods of presentation. An edition can be designed that will be available—that is, intelligible without the need for laborious and sophisticated prior analysis—to a circle of musicians wider than a small group of specialists; and the edition need not compromise scholarly standards, as Nottebohm's publications did. In particular, the relation of the editor's transcription to the original source is made quite clear, which is a prime requirement. A certain amount of preliminary interpretation can be conceded, and justified by the fact that the facsimile is there as an objective 'control'.

Thus the present transcription supplies (in square brackets or with some other typographical distinction) key and time signatures and other details omitted by Beethoven, and normalizes the notation to facilitate reading. (We are close to Schmitz in this regard, and somewhat more liberal than Fishman.) In addition, and this is of course more significant, an attempt has been made to isolate the sketches from one another, and to group them under the works and movements to which the sketches refer. This procedure has the disadvantage of obscuring the context of the sketches in their original setting, a disadvantage that would be very serious were it not for the presence of the facsimile which sets forth this context accurately. On the other hand, the procedure has the advantage of placing the sketches in the context of the compositional process in which they form a stage, and for which they presumably hold our interest in the first place. Most Beethoven sketchbooks contain so dense an accumulation of sketches for a few works that even after the material has been isolated and reordered, the picture remains highly complex. However, the London miscellany has no works sketched for more than a few pages. Many works are sketched quite briefly. In this relatively simple situation, reordering the sketches is an obvious and effective means of clarification. It may also be observed that since more often than not the order of the pages in the miscellany is arbitrary, little would be saved beyond the *status quo* by preserving this particular order.

As has been remarked above, the system of isolating and rearranging certain sketches represents a first step towards interpretation, over and above simple transcription. It might be argued that the information involved should be provided in editorial notes rather than incorporated within the edition itself. But although this would be a possible procedure, in the editor's view it would militate against the intelligibility and utility of the publication in a decisive way. The information would be effectively buried, and could be applied only as the result of cumbersome labour which, it may be suspected, readers would be slow to undertake (and which they might reasonably have expected an editor to have saved them). On the other hand, with the large number of smaller, obscure sketches and miscellaneous notations, comprising about a third of the manuscript, no effort has been made to put them into any special order. They are presented in part 2 of the transcription in the sequence of the manuscript, folio by folio, though here too the notations have been isolated from one another, a process that cannot always be carried out with complete objectivity. Here as in part 1 of the transcription, the editorial decisions on such and other matters can all be checked against the facsimile.

* * *

Beethoven's handwriting was notoriously bad. Max Unger prefaced his valuable monograph on *Beethovens Handschrift* with the composer's own acknowledgement of this fact, in a letter of 1813 to his friend Zmeskall:

> Dear good Z. Don't be annoyed if I ask you to write the enclosed *Adresse* on the enclosed letter; the person whom the letter is for is always complaining that no letters come from me; yesterday I took a letter to the post, where they asked me where the letter was supposed to go?—so I see that my handwriting is perhaps misunderstood as often as I am myself . . .[3]

Misunderstandings have continued to be common, as scholars have puzzled over the often intractable marks made by Beethoven's pen. If this is true of autographs and letters written for the benefit of copyists and correspondents, it is certainly even more true of sketches and inscriptions in sketchbooks, which Beethoven wrote only for himself.

However, the puzzles are considerably less formidable in the period represented by the London miscellany than in later years. Age, confidence, increasing boldness of musical imagination, deepening psychological stress—all these factors took their toll on legibility. Beethoven's early hand is characterized by Winternitz as 'speedy and thin but fairly clear', by Unger as '*passabel*';[4] compared with the decipherment of later sketchbooks and letters, reading the miscellany is a relatively feasible matter. Many of the Bonn pages have an almost copy-book appearance, and even the early Vienna pages—which begin to look more characteristic—count as relatively well spaced, coherent, clear, and sometimes even neat. There is a considerable difference, of course, between the legibility of autographs and sketches, and between sketches done at Beethoven's normal high speed and those done in a particular hurry. None the less, neither the impetuous sprawl of the writing itself, nor the confusing complex of shorthand and elision, nor the merciless jumbling

xiv

of various ideas on a single page, reaches the level that has to be expected in the period after 1800.

The best introduction to Beethoven's handwriting is the monograph by Unger already mentioned, though in its thirty-two pages it can convey only a fraction of what the author must have learned ultimately during a long career dealing with Beethoven autographs. The following brief remarks supplement Unger's observations with special reference to aspects of the early sketches.

Beethoven generally omitted clefs, key and time signatures, but these can almost always be supplied safely with the help of the accidentals. On the whole, accidentals are indicated adequately—and sometimes Beethoven takes surprising pains, as for example in long chromatic scale passages. Precautionary accidentals are rather common. In many cases accidentals appear to hold not only for the bar in which they are written but also for the next bar. Rhythm too is usually indicated with reasonable clarity, though Beethoven sometimes confuses quavers and crotchets, and shows a pardonable impatience with the exact notation of demisemi- and hemidemisemiquavers. Triplets are rarely marked with a '3'; persistent dotted passages may appear in even notes; dots and barlines are not infrequently omitted. Minim and semibreve rests look the same—as might be expected—and in the transcription the attempt has not generally been made to distinguish them. Quaver rests can sometimes be mistaken for crotchets or quaver flags.

More troublesome is the notation of pitch. When sketching rapidly, Beethoven did not take the time to write note heads for black notes, and even when a dot or a little backwards hook per-

---

[3] Max Unger, *Beethovens Handschrift* (*Veröffentlichungen des Beethovenhauses in Bonn*, iv), Bonn, 1926, p. 5. The letter is Anderson 434, 9 Oct. 1813 (freshly translated).
[4] Emanuel Winternitz, *Musical Autographs from Monteverdi to Hindemith*, 1955, 2nd edn., New York, 1965, i. 83; Unger, op. cit. 6.

forms such a function, it often appears imperfectly placed in respect to the lines and spaces. As an example, a case may be considered in which the headless stem of a downward note just reaches up to and touches the top line of the staff. In the treble clef, this could be an F written low which has not quite crossed its line, or an E which fills its space only too well, or a D fixed on the second line and extending up further than it should. (It could also be a G written too low; Beethoven had a tendency to miss on the low side.) In an isolated instance, it may be impossible to tell the pitch within two or three scale degrees.

The situation is rarely as desperate as this, however, since there are several factors that allow closer determination: (1) the presence of accidentals, which usually admit of only one interpretation, (2) the relative height of adjacent notes; in a scale passage, for example, some notes may be ambiguously placed on the staff but aligned with their neighbours clearly enough to make Beethoven's intention manifest, (3) the general musical sense of the passage involved, and (4) comparison with other parts of the same sketch, or related sketches, or the final version of the work in question. It is obvious that particular care is necessary in applying the latter two criteria if all irregularities, solecisms, and changes of conception are not to be smoothed out. But musical considerations cannot be ruled out in transcribing music, and if handled with caution these criteria are certainly admissible and very helpful.

In preparing the transcription, it seemed pointless to signal in the critical notes or elsewhere every crotchet and quaver that stands slightly out of alignment or admits of several readings. The procedure followed in this edition is to note the literal manuscript reading only when it differs decidedly from the proposed transcription. We may return to the example given above, with the note stem touching the top line in the treble clef. If the pitch is considered to be either F, E, or D, this edition transcribes it as such without further comment; in short, if Beethoven's wayward notation for pitch can be construed to fit the note that is thought to be intended, the edition prints the note without discussing whether the end of the stem might perhaps be *closer* to some other pitch. However, if the intended pitch is thought to be G, the edition prints this G with a small italic *e* above it, signifying that the most 'normal' reading of the manuscript, in the abstract, would be E. Italic letters of this sort are provided when and only when the notation is unambiguously off, though complete consistency in this matter is probably not possible. More dubious cases are noted in the transcription by question marks.

Pitch notation of black notes on the staff is the most ambiguous; notation of chords, black notes on ledger lines, and white notes is less so. None the less, it will probably be found that even these categories cause more problems in reading than does, for example, the notation of rhythm. Beethoven's own problem in this regard is indicated by his not infrequent resort to clarifying letters over ambiguous notes.

Among the most common abbreviations is 'bis', often very roughly scrawled, always under an arc. ('Ter' also appears on one page.) The letters 'u. s. w.' for 'und so weiter' are ubiquitous; apparently Beethoven did not begin using 'etc.' until the end of the 1790s (see ff. 152^v and 162^r). In Bonn manuscripts, fractions are occasionally used to correct rhythms, e.g. '$\frac{1}{4}$' will correct a quaver into a crotchet (*Viertelnote*). A variety of indications is found for cross-reference purposes: 'Vi:' referring to ':de', and pairs of crosses, signs, letters, and numbers such as 'N', 'No', '20', 'N 1000', and others. Generally these simply point to another part of the page, or another page; Beethoven has run out of space and still wishes to continue, or he has come back to a hemmed-in sketch and wishes to record an afterthought. But sometimes the marks seem to indicate a cut, an insert, a correction, or a variant, and sometimes only one of the pair of marks can be found. Their import is not always clear.

The reading of Beethoven's writing of words, texts, and inscriptions presents its own severe problems. For the student who is not a native German, there are the added difficulties of interpreting unusual contractions, and wrestling with the composer's not infrequent quirks or plain errors of spelling and grammar. The editor has therefore felt especially fortunate to have obtained expert assistance in this area, as has already been stated in the Acknowledgements, from Professor Spahr and Dr. Weise. Every inscription, indeed every random letter on the manuscript page may have an important bearing on the musical material: in particular, on the continuity or sequence of this material, and its identification. For these are two topics that still remain to be investigated after the music has been read. (Though in fact they are not strictly to be separated from the reading; the reading is sometimes helped by hypotheses about continuity, or by comparison with the work that has been identified.) Determining the sequence of the writings is a major difficulty, as has already been pointed out earlier in this introduction. There are many situations in which one cannot be sure whether a particular sketch was written before or after another in the vicinity—or indeed whether it was all written at the same time, rather than revised or extended on another occasion. Usually Beethoven wrote from the top of the page down, of course, but he left spaces when he thought an idea might call for continuation later; and if it did not, he still tended to use up the blank space with other material. This is not to speak of those pages apparently dashed off at a high pitch of excitement, with every last modicum of space returned to and filled in to the point of anarchy. The

xvi

sequence of writing may be revealed by spacing that is unusually cramped or spread out, or by the aspect of the pens and inks. Except in the more obvious instances, however, the editor has had little success in distinguishing inks, mainly because even ink of a single kind often appears to have dried at different colours, making judgements about new inks hazardous. It is possible that this question would yield to more refined methods of analysis than the editor has been able to bring to it. A final word of caution is necessary about possible breaks that may occur without notice within drafts that seem to be continuous. As a rule, breaks are indicated by a 'u. s. w.' or a space; but all rules concerning Beethoven's sketches have their exceptions.

In the matter of identification of the sketches, an edition of the London miscellany can rely to a considerable extent on the researches of Nottebohm and Shedlock. They identified most of the important works sketched, as is set forth fully in the notes on the individual works, pp. 275–91. Shedlock also allowed himself to speculate about a number of conjectural relationships between sketches and finished works; perhaps inevitably, some of his suggestions have been repeated without an indication of their hypothetical nature, which Shedlock was always careful to state. This is a little unfortunate, but none the less such hypothetical identifications are always worth considering, even if it is found that the evidence for them is insufficient. A number of new identifications, both firm and conjectural, have been made in the course of preparing the present edition. It is unfortunately probable that still others have been overlooked; the editor will be grateful to learn of these from readers.

*　　　*　　　*

To the acknowledgements made earlier, I wish to add another, at once deeper and more remote, to my former teacher and dear friend the late Dr. Erich Hertzmann, Professor of Music at Columbia University. His influence on the present edition may be counted both general and specific. Born at Krefeld in the Rhineland, not too far distant from Bonn, Hertzmann left Germany in the 1930s, one of a group of refugee scholars who were to play a leading role in the development of musicology in America. More particularly, having a lifelong interest in and encyclopedic knowledge of the Beethoven sketches, he expounded their mysteries to a generation of students at Columbia and Princeton Universities. I very much regret that he could not see this edition, which directly reflects his inspiration and his teaching.

JOSEPH KERMAN

INDEX OF WORKS COPIED OR SKETCHED

Folio numbers are printed in bold type when the folios contain autographs, in ordinary
type when they contain sketches

Part 1

AUTOGRAPHS, SKETCHES, AND DRAFTS

WORKS WITH OPUS NUMBER

WORKS WITHOUT OPUS NUMBER (WoO)

OTHER WORKS

NOTE ON THE TRANSCRIPTION

The beginning of each new sketch is preceded by a reference to its location in the manuscript, consisting of folio number, staff number, and bar number (omitted when the bar number is bar 1). Thus $^{69r}_1$ signifies f. 69 recto, staff 1, bar 1, and $^{116v}_{8/2}$ signifies f. 116 verso, staff 8, bar 2. When no reference of this kind appears at the beginning of a line, the music is to be understood as continuing directly from a previous line. A new staff number is noted on the transcription, above or below the staff, to show each point at which a sketch proceeds from one staff in the manuscript to another. In counting bars, initial fractional bars are omitted, and no restitution is made in cases where obvious bar lines may have been left out.

Material added by the editor is distinguished by means of square brackets (for notes, clefs, signatures, song texts, etc., as well as editorial captions), dotted lines (bar lines and ties), or small music type (rests, accidentals, and precautionary accidentals). Where manuscript readings have been emended, original rhythms are shown by indications such as 'ms: ♫', original pitches by small italic letters (*e, f*) next to the emended notes. (Letters in bold type such as **e, f, fis**, however, are Beethoven's own.) Doubtful readings are pointed out by question marks. The spacing of the notes and the direction of their stems have been normalized without special comment.

In cases of cancellation or alteration, the original version is given in small music type or ordinary type with cancellation lines through it. A mark (⫲) has been devised to indicate illegible cancellations.

Piano Trio in G, Op. 1 No. 2: Adagio — Allegro vivace

★ *semiquaver beam cancelled*

Largo con espressione

★ *the rhythmic notation for this and similar figures is inconsistent and open to several interpretations. It has not been emended in the transcription.*

Scherzo. Allegro (piano score – fragment)

Finale. Presto

oder weiter ausgeführt

Piano Trio in C minor, Op. 1 No. 3: Allegro con brio

Menuetto. Quasi allegro

Finale. Prestissimo

Sonata in F for Violoncello and Piano, Op. 5 No. 1: Adagio sostenuto — Allegro

Rondo. Allegro vivace

Sonata in G minor for Violoncello and Piano, Op. 5 No. 2: Allegro molto più tosto presto

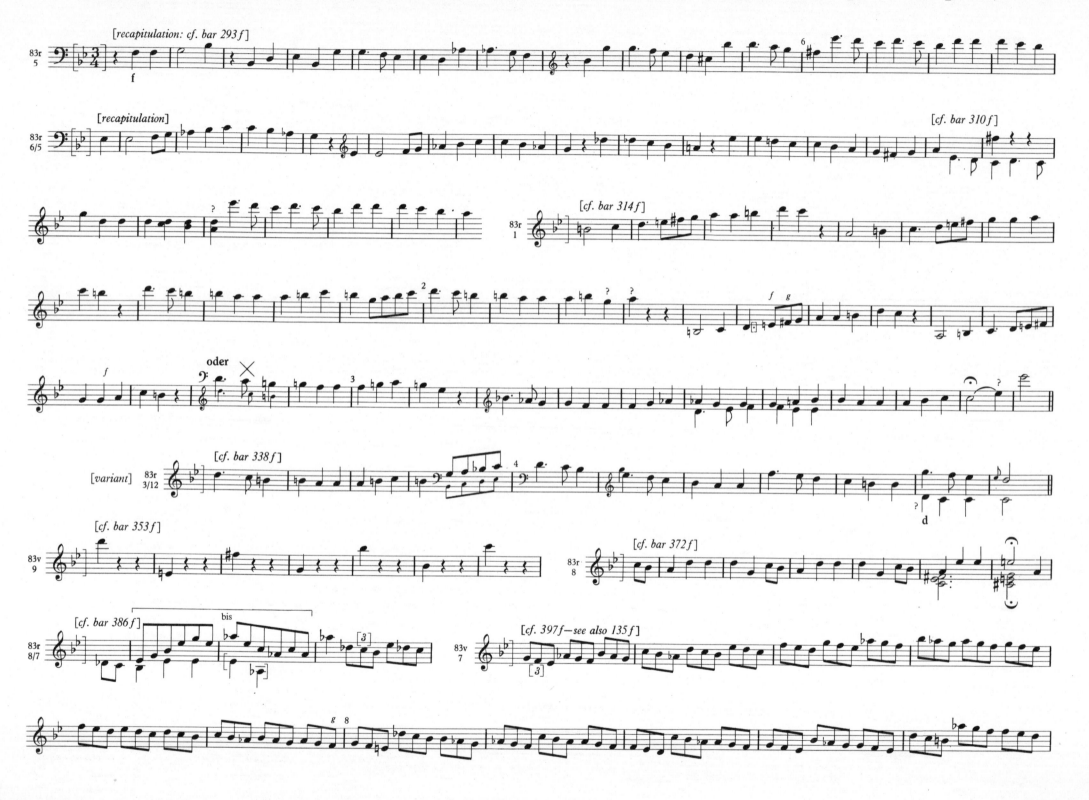

Rondo. Allegro

★ *originally written in the bass clef; the first treble clef and the '8' were added later.*

Sonata in D for Piano, Four Hands, Op. 6: Rondo. Moderato

★ *in the ms, these passages are all in quaver values.*

† *from f. 110v, 1*

Piano Sonata in E♭, Op. 7: Allegro

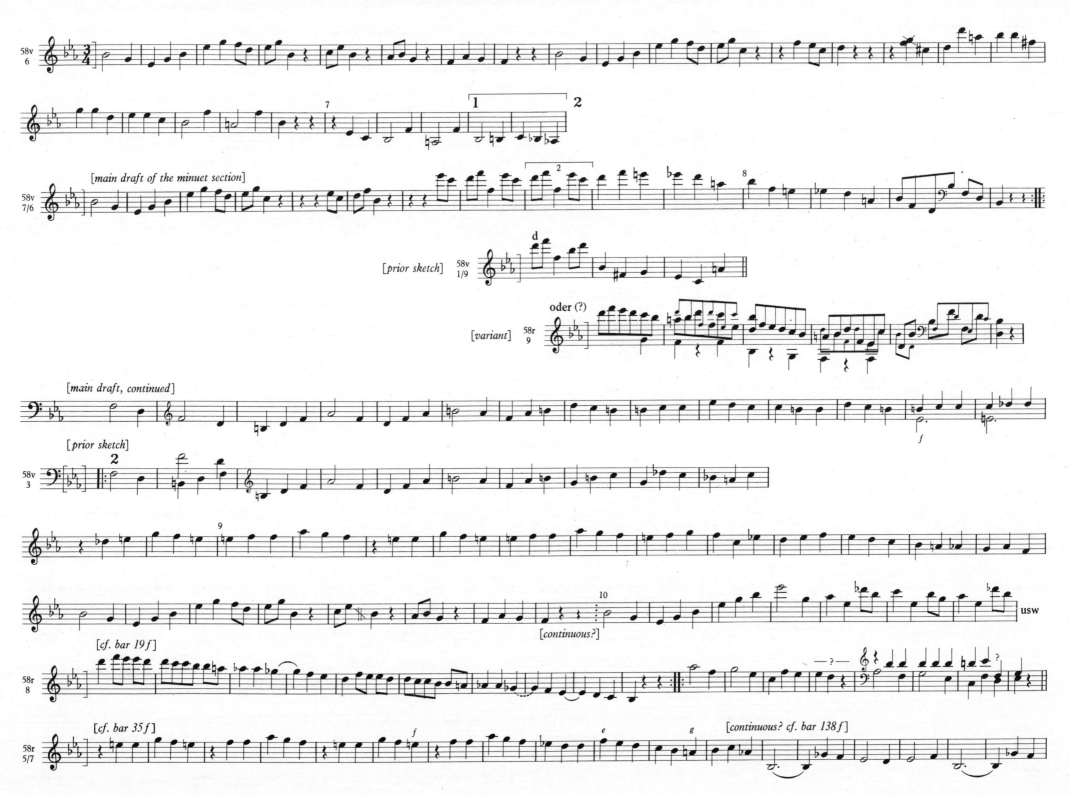

13

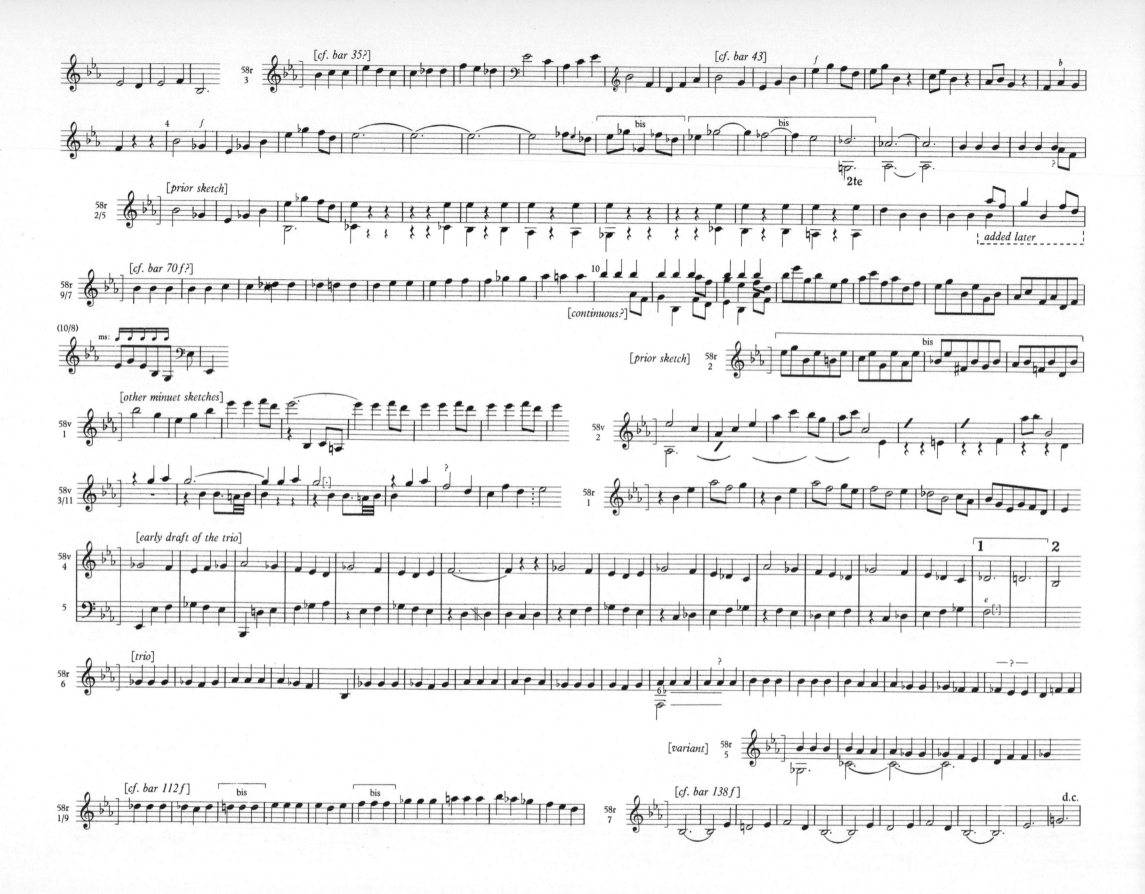

Serenade for String Trio, Op. 8: Marcia. Allegro

Adagio

Adagio, ma non tanto e cantabile

Finale

★ *semiquaver beam cancelled*

Piano Sonata in F, Op. 10 No. 2: Allegro

Allegretto

Presto

Piano Sonata in D, Op. 10 No. 3: Presto

[abbreviated draft, from the end of the exposition to the conclusion]

20

Largo e mesto

Menuetto. Allegro

Rondo. Allegro

Trio for Clarinet, Violoncello, and Piano, Op. 11: Allegro con brio

Adagio

★ *a variant for the preceding bar, or for the one above (bar 8 of sketch)*

Piano Sonata in C minor, Op. 13 ('Pathétique'): Rondo. Allegro

Piano Sonata in E, Op. 14 No. 1: Allegro

Exposition Sketches

26

Development Sketches

2ter Theil [see p. 27, line 11]

122v
5/6

122v
8

usw ohne das the[ma] durchzuführen
bis nach dem ✕

122v
14

122v
17

[variants] 122v
16/5

18/10

Sketches for the Recapitulation and Coda

[cf. bar 93 f]

121r
16

17

[complete recapitulation and coda]

★ [three sketches for the coda]

★ an illegible word or abbreviation. In these sketches, not all the crotchets are dotted in the ms.

Allegretto

Rondo. Allegro comodo

[early ideas for the finale?]

in gis moll
E dur
adagio
$\frac{6}{8}$ tel takt

★ *in the ms most of the minims lack dots.*

32

33

Piano Concerto in C, Op. 15: Allegro con brio

★ *an extra sharp in the ms.*

★ *in the ms, this clef appears at the beginning of the bar.*   † *quaver beam cancelled*

36

Largo

Rondo. Allegro scherzando

Quintet for Wind Instruments and Piano, Op. 16: Grave — Allegro, ma non troppo

Andante cantabile

40

Rondo. Allegro ma non troppo

String Quartet in A, Op. 18 No. 5: Andante cantabile

Allegro

Piano Concerto in B♭, Op. 19: Allegro con brio

Adagio

127v, 5/6: **Concerto in B dur adagio in d dur** [*an early idea for Op. 19?*]

*an illegible word; evidently this bar was to be expanded to two.

49

50

Rondo. Molto allegro

Early Phase (ff. 147–148)

[draft: exposition—bridge and second group]

[sic]

[second theme—early attempt]

erstemal (?)

[variant]

[shorter sketches: first group]

bis

[tutti]

[variant]

★ possibly a cut between the two signs

52

Intermediate Phase (f. 97)

★ *i.e. repeat from 𝄋 ?*　　　† *a second ending, for the point marked ⊕ ?*

Late Phase (ff. 64—65)

an illegible word   † *the superfluous clefs may indicate new starts after omissions.*

★ *these series of crotchets are not dotted in the ms.*

★ *the two rests are reversed.*

57

Piano Concerto in C minor, Op. 37: Allegro con brio

Rondo. Allegro

Adelaide ('Einsam wandelt dein Freund'), Op. 46

- de!   Einst, o Wun-der!   einst, o Wun-der!   o Wun-der! ach, ent-

-blüht auf mei-nem Gra-be   ei-ne Blu-me der A-sche mei-nes Her-zens;   deut-lich

schimmert, deut-lich schimmert auf je-dem Pur-pur-blättchen, auf je-dem Pur-pur-blätt-chen: A-dela-i-de!

A-- de-la-i-de!   deutlich schimmert, deutlich schimmert auf je-dem Pur-pur-blätt-chen, auf je-dem

Pur-pur-blätt-chen: A-de-la-i-de!   A-de-la-i-de!]

44v
12/9
[variant]
13/3
a-- -de-la-i-de

44r [cf. bar 74 f]
9
[o] wun-der ent-blüht auf mei-nem gra-[be]

44v [cf. bar 86 f]
12/3
ei-ne blu-[me...]

44r [cf. bar 96 f?]
10
deut-lich schimert auf je-dem (?) pur-pur-[blättchen...]

Sonatina in G minor for Piano, Op. 49 No. 1: Andante

Sonatine

par l. v. Bthvn.

66r
1
2

Sonatina in G for Piano, Op. 49 No. 2: Allegro ma non troppo

★ *ms: an extra quaver A*   † *semiquaver beam cancelled*

Tempo di Menuetto

Feuerfarb' ('Ich weiss eine Farbe'), Op. 52 No. 2

Feuerfarb.

[Ich weiss ei-ne Far-be, der bin ich so hold, die ach-te ich hö-her als Sil-ber und Gold, die trag' ich so gerne um

Stirn und Ge-wand und ha-be sie 'Far-be der Wahrheit' ge-nannt.   Wohl blü-het in lieb-li-cher, sanf-ter Ge-stalt die glü-hen-de Rose, doch]

[earlier version on staffs 8-9 and 11-12]

Das Liedchen von der Ruhe ('Im Arm der Liebe'), Op. 52 No. 3

★ *the brackets are in the ms.*

'Ah! perfido', Scena and Aria for Soprano, Op. 65

★ *probably a crotchet G♯*   † *the hyphens in 'dite' are in the ms.*

Variations on Mozart's 'Ein Mädchen oder Weibchen', for Violoncello and Piano, Op. 66

Sextet for Wind Instruments, Op. 71: Menuetto. Quasi allegretto

68

Rondo. Allegro

Flohlied ('Es war einmal ein König'), Op. 75 No. 3

Da miss dem jun - ker Klei - der da miss ihm ho - sen an

Rondo in B♭ for Piano and Orchestra, WoO 6

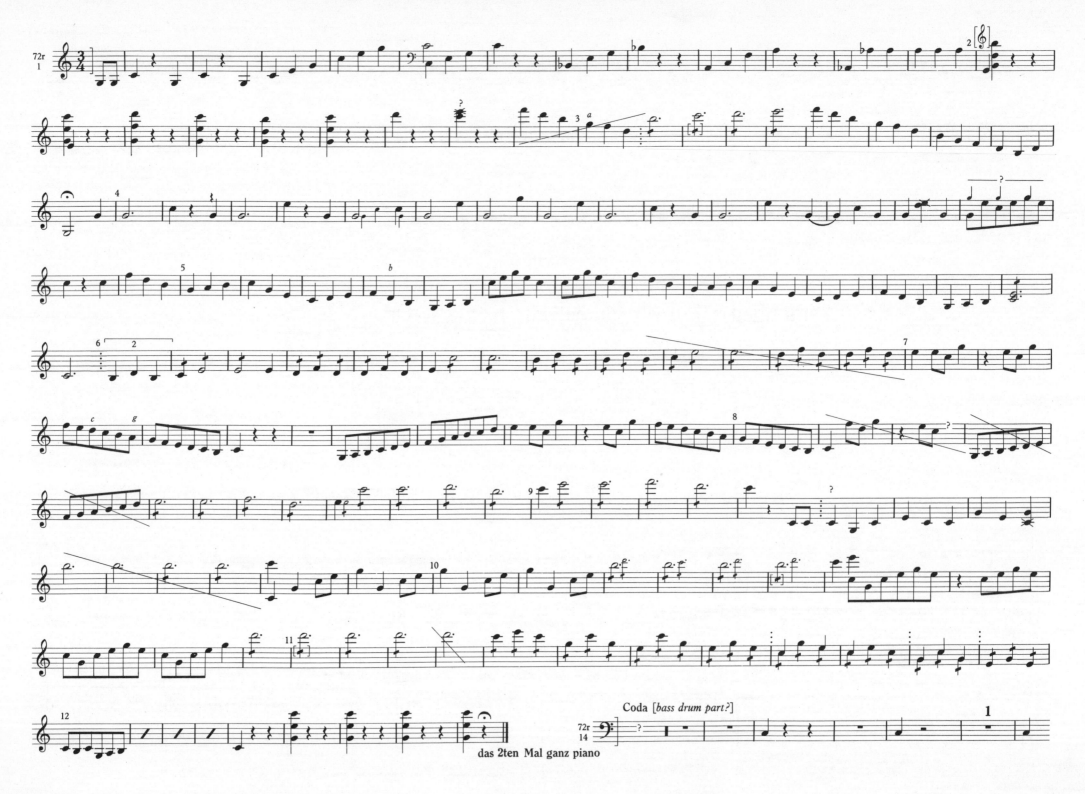

das 2ten Mal ganz piano

Coda [*bass drum part?*]

Seven Ländler, WoO 11

Twelve Allemandes for Orchestra, WoO 13

Twelve Contredanses for Orchestra, WoO 14

Duo for Viola and Violoncello, WoO 32

Duett mit zwei obligaten Augengläsern von L. v. Beethoven.

74

★ *the first rewriting (staffs 13-14) is cancelled. The second rewriting (staffs 15-16) was also cancelled,*
but then reinstated by a 'gut'; but it is uncertain whether the reinstatement applies to the last bar.

[sketch]

★ms: an extra crotchet rest in both parts

trio

[*sketch for another movement ?*]

c.p.

79

Sonatina in C minor for Mandoline and Piano, WoO 43a

Sonatina per il Mandolino. Composta da l. v. Beethoven

Adagio in E♭ for Mandoline and Piano, WoO 43b

★ *in the ms, the natural appears one note too soon.*

Sonatina in C for Mandoline and Piano, WoO 44a

Andante and Variations in D for Mandoline and Piano, WoO 44b

Allegretto in C minor for Piano, WoO 53 (Hess 66)

Variations on 'Venni amore' by Righini, for Piano, WoO 65

Variations on a Theme by Count Waldstein, for Piano, Four Hands, WoO 67

★ *most of the triplets are written as semiquavers.*

88

Variations on a Russian Dance from Wranitzky's *Das Waldmädchen*, for Piano, WoO 71

Variations on 'God save the King', for Piano, WoO 78 (?)

Cantata for the Elevation of Leopold II, WoO 88: 'Fliesse, Wonnezähre, fliesse!', Aria for Soprano

89

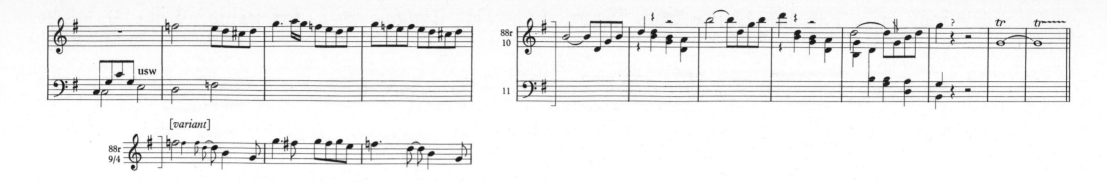

'Mit Mädeln sich vertragen', Aria for Bass, WoO 90

'Primo amore', Rondo for Soprano, WoO 92

Trinklied ('Erhebt das Glas'), WoO 109

★ *perhaps originally A C ♪ here, obliterated*

★ *perhaps originally A C ♪ here, obliterated*

92

Der Freie Mann ('Wer ist ein freier Mann?'), WoO 117 (Hess 146)

[Der Freie Mann, Hess 146]

★ *these rests transmit the earliest version.*

Der Freje Mann [WoO 117]

★ No 4.

1 B

★ *ties across the barline have been scratched out and the staff lines inked over.*

Seufzer eines Ungeliebten und Gegenliebe ('Hast du nicht Liebe zugemessen'), WoO 118

'O care selve', WoO 119

Opferlied ('Die Flamme lodert'), WoO 126 (Hess 145)

Allemandes and Contredanses

★ *these words and phrases appear at the bottom of the page and may not refer specifically to the musical segments above them.*

★ ms: a superfluous crotchet rest.

Cadenza in G for Piano

in ottava

★ *an extra C in the ms.*

Canon 'Meine Herren' (cf. Canon 'Herr Graf', Hess 276)

Canon in A

Composition (cantata?) in B♭

Klawier quintett mit concertant Violin accompagnement von 2 oboe, 2 fagotti, 2 Corni ★

★ this remark, at the bottom of the page, may not refer to this composition.   † see note on p. 285.

Composition (bagatelle?) in C for Piano

Composition (rondo?) in C for Piano

★ *ms: semiquaver beam cancelled?*

Composition (rondo?) in D for Piano

schluss *ff*

f

[*p*]

[*f*]

usw

bis

7/7

[3]

[*continuous?*]

[3]

8/7

im Rondo
des
Conzerts
eine
Fuge.

zu No 30
Mineur
wenn dieses
Stück im
es versezt
wird.

53v
15

ff

f

f

16

8va

usw

53v
15/12

16/12

★ *these rests appear to be repeated in the ms.*

Composition in D for Orchestra

★ *in the ms, the last two quavers are to the right of the barline.* † *or tr ?*

Composition (fantasia?) in D major/minor for Piano

[variant]

★ *the following eight bars were expanded from an original four.*

Variants to the first allegro

[cf. p. 113, brace 4, bar 10]

[cf. p. 113, brace 5, bar 12]

★ *no beams in the ms.*

★ *apparently a rewriting of the previous bar but one (which was not cancelled, however) and a substitute for the new*
theme which was begun in the left hand (also not cancelled).

119

★ *a key signature of four flats has been added later here.*

★ *the revision of the previous bars was evidently designed to avoid this sharp, but it is not cancelled.*

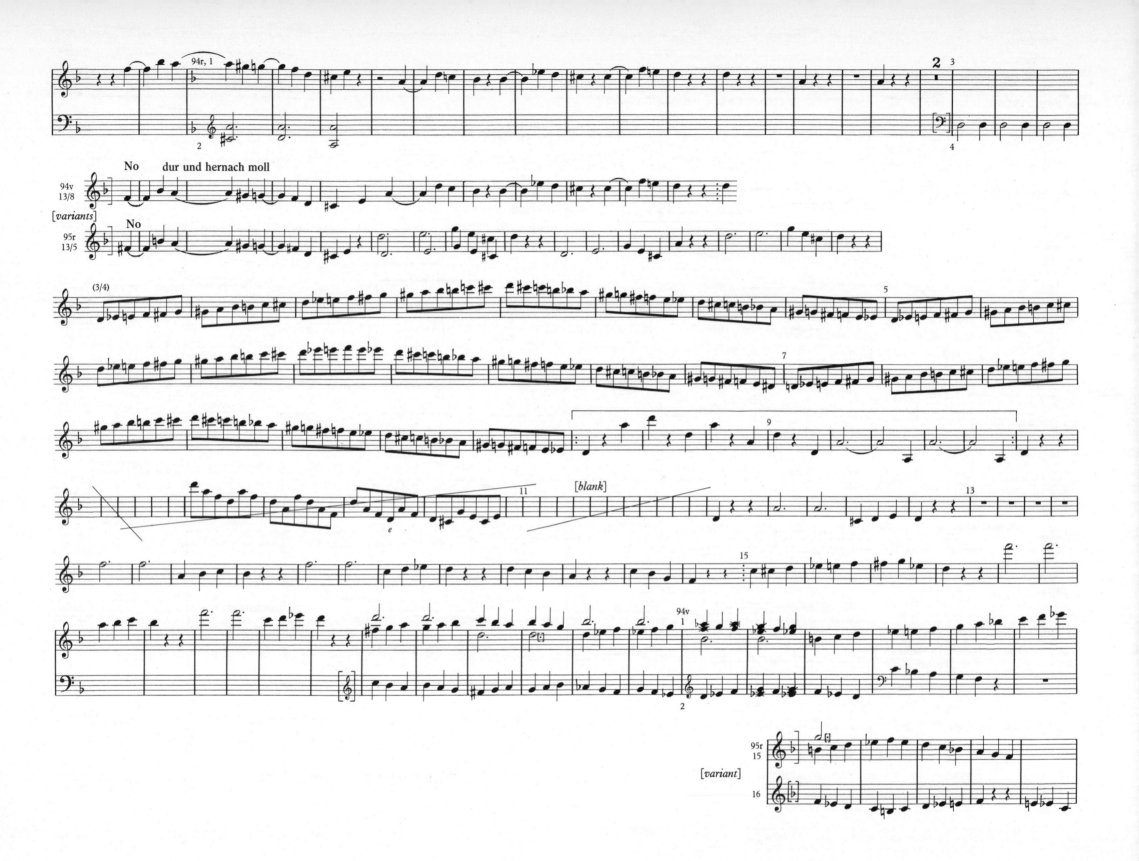

★ *these bass arpeggios may not go with the right hand; they may be part of a rejected earlier version.*

Variants to the second allegro

Composition in G for Orchestra: Oboe Part (by Beethoven?)

★ *for the points marked × near the end? cf. also p. 122, staff 5.*   † *possibly continuous with the variant on p. 122, staff 4.*

Concerto in F for Oboe, Hess 12: Slow Movement

Concerto in A for Piano: Adagio in D

Duo in E♭ for Violin and Violoncello (fragment)

★ an extra crotchet rest in the ms.   *† bowing and staccato marks stop at this point.*

Fugue in C for Keyboard, Hess 64

ma Chi tutto può far que ✗ etc

Lamentations of Jeremiah

★apparently figured from B♮

Minuet in F for Orchestra

Quartet (?) in G for Wind Instruments and Piano: Allegro

134

Adagio (?)

Finale: Variations on 'Ah, vous dirai-je, maman'

136

Romance in E minor for Flute, Bassoon, Piano, and Orchestra, Hess 13 (fragment)

★ *the small notes here indicate not an earlier version, but a later addition in a fine pen. The changes are not incorporated into the parallel passage at bars 37—43.*

★ *the small notes here indicate not an earlier version, but a later addition in a fine pen. The changes are not incorporated into the parallel passage at bars 37—43.*

segue maggiore

144

Rondo in A for Violin and Piano

★ *these sf marks are so placed in the ms.*

Sonata Movement in C (i)

Sonata Movement in C (ii)*

* other notations on ff. 150—151 may refer to this movement: see pp. 262—4.   † in the ms, this sharp appears to the left of the prior note.

149

Sonata Movement in C minor (i)

Preliminary Sketches

150

Early Phase

★ *the fermata and the next bar were probably added later, when Beethoven cancelled the rest of staff 9. Presumably he also meant to cancel staff 10.*

Intermediate Phase

Later Phase

★ *a smudged treble clef?* † *originally minims or dotted minims.*

‡ *presumably the da capo encompasses the first theme, i.e., 18 bars from the beginning of the draft.*

155

Sonata Movement in C minor (ii: by Beethoven?)

Sonata Movement in Eb

★ *in the ms, this sign appears in the next bar.*   † *ms: semiquavers*

Song in C (i)

da das lied nur allejahr einmal gemach[t] wird, so darf es schon etwas schwehr sejn

★ *minim stem cancelled*

Song in C (ii)

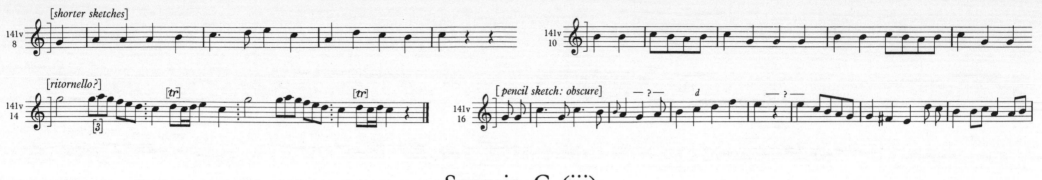

Song in C (iii)

Song in E♭

Song in G (i: 'Ich sah sie heut'')

ich sah sie heut o lie – be! Wie war das Mäd-chen schön da wollt ich was ich füh – le ihr oh – ne scham ge – stehen

Song in G (ii)

[sketches for the beginning?]

[draft encompassing most of the song?]

Ri[tornello]

oder d moll

dir

so vor lie – be

rito[rnello]

wo von

★ *possibly some letters here*

★ in the ms, the sharp appears to the left of the barline.

Song in G (iii)

an Gott ist dieses wenn ich mich recht ist besinne

★ *a large space in the ms; the sketch may not be continuous.*

Study (?) in A♭ for Piano

★ *the D♭s were added later.*   † *the ms reads A C E, evidently the chord for the repetition of bar 1.*   ‡ *the D♮s may be cancelled.*

Study in B♭ for Piano, Hess 58

Symphony in C: Introduction—Allegro

★ *in the ms, this rest appears to the right of the barline.*

★ *minim stem cancelled*

★ *minim stem cancelled*   † *the main theme has probably been elided here; cf. p. 172, staff 1.*   ‡ *beam cancelled*

Definitive Phase

★ *in this score many of the minim and semibreve rests are carelessly placed.*

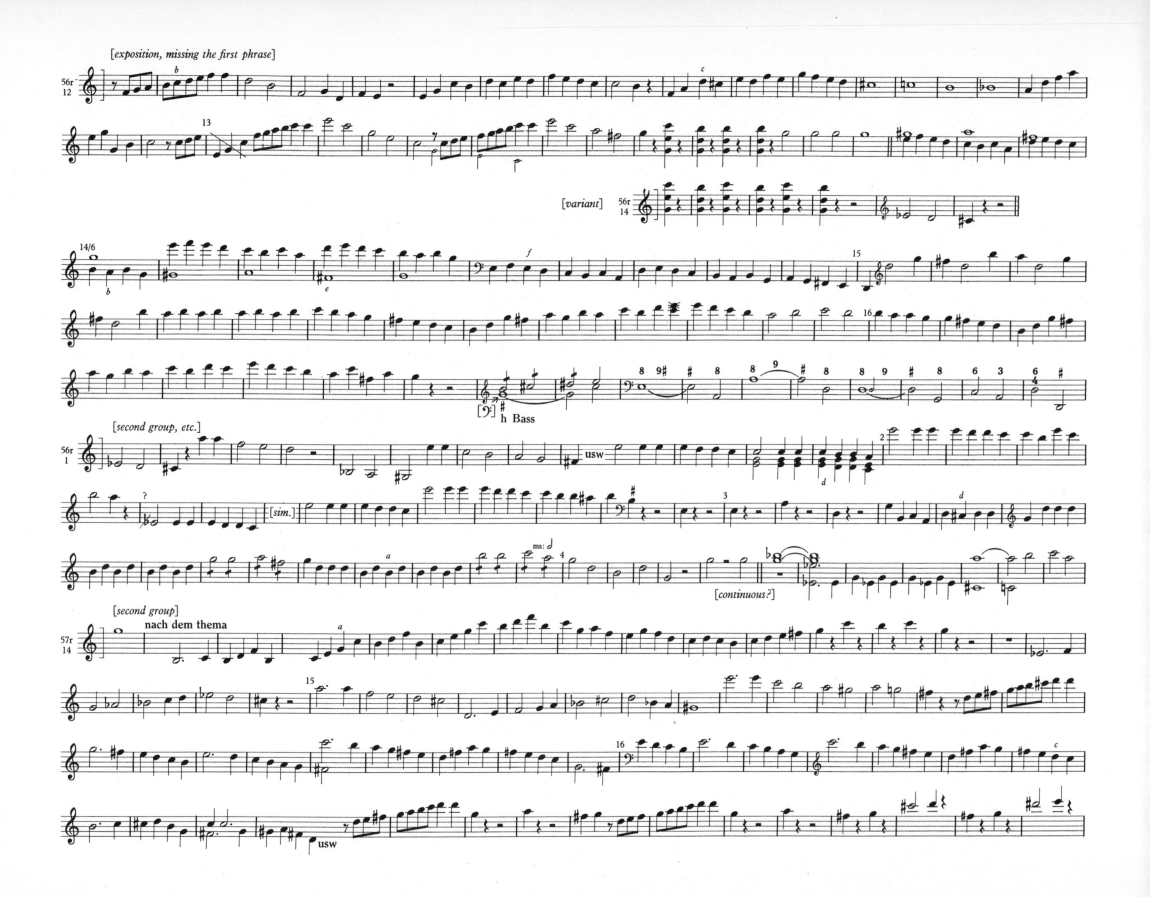

170

★ *originally minims (?)*

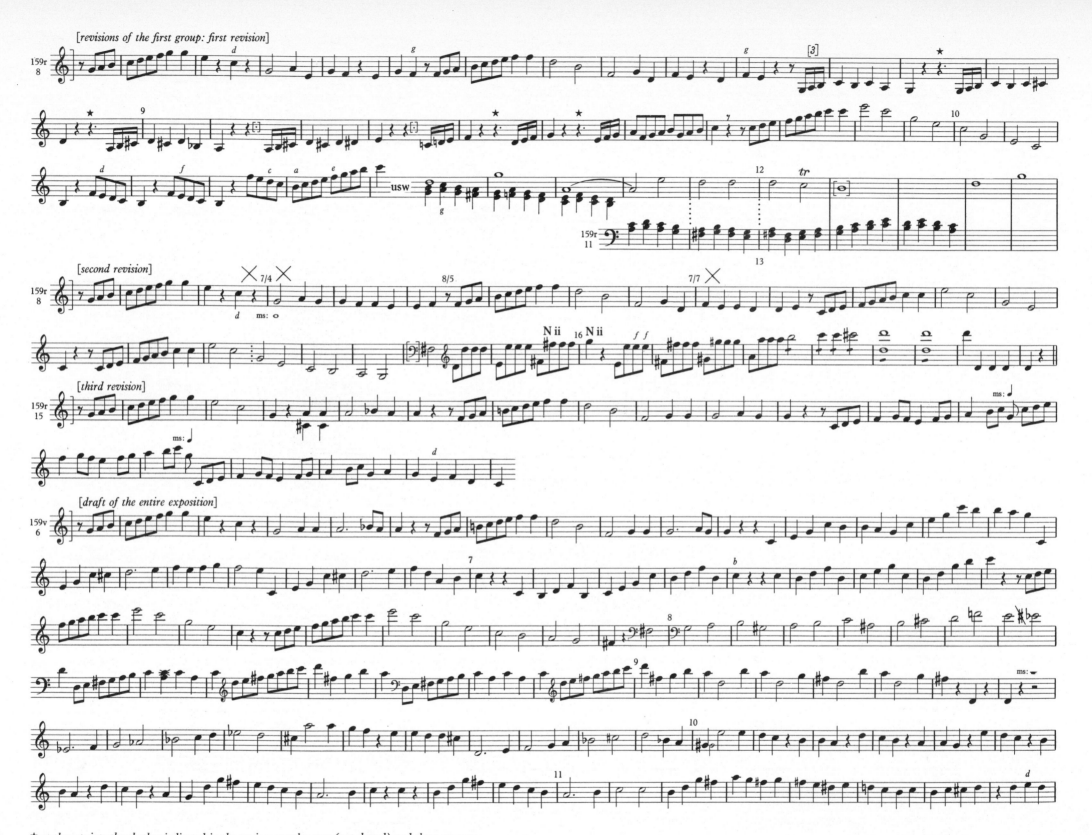

★ *at these points the rhythm indicated in the ms is a crotchet rest (not dotted) and three quavers.*

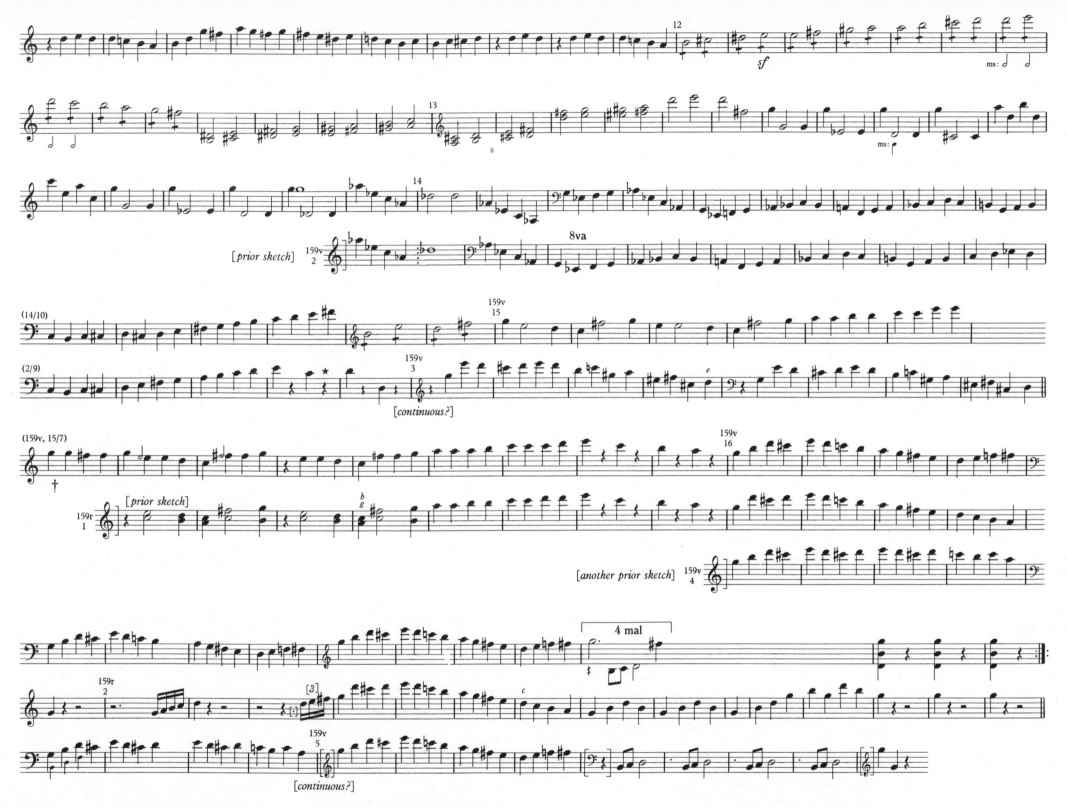

★ *in the ms, the rest appears to the right of the barline.* † *possibly a revision of the previous 7 bars*

Minuet★

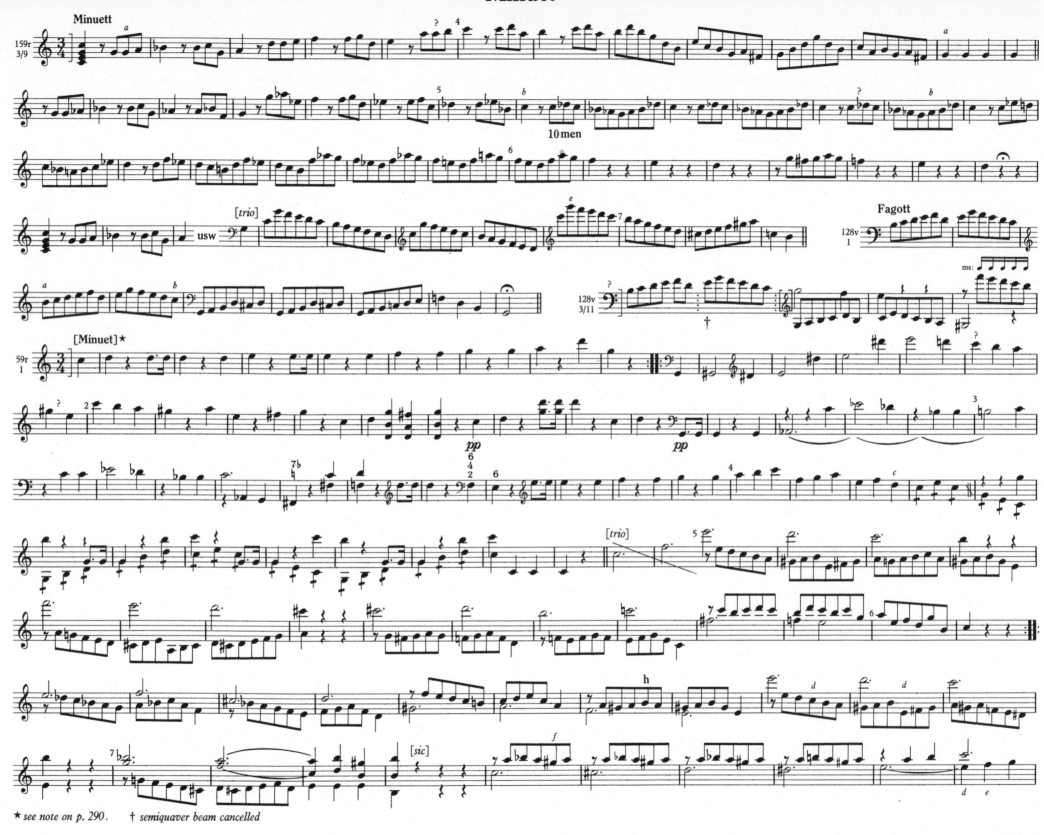

★ *see note on p. 290.*   † *semiquaver beam cancelled*

Symphony in C minor, Hess 298

Sinfonia

★ *see notes on p. 291.*

Symphony Slow Movement in E

★ *demisemiquaver beam cancelled*   † *or A♯?*

Zum andante [*for the 'sinfonia', when transposed to F?*]

Mineu[r]

2tes Mineur

Piano Trio in E♭: Allegretto, Hess 48 (fragment)

[Alle]gretto

[Violin]

[Violoncello]

[Piano]

in ottava

★ *semiquaver beam cancelled*

*originally ♪♫♪

[torn]

Variations on Mozart's 'Là ci darem la mano', for Violoncello and Piano (?)

Part 2

SHORTER SKETCHES, EXERCISES,
AND MISCELLANEOUS NOTATIONS

f. 39

see also
p. 161

Hie[r]bei muss der 3te Finger über dem 4ten solange kreuzweiss liegen,
bis dieser wegzieht und alsdann der 3te an seine Stelle kömmt.

Andante

linke Hand

accorde

★ ms: demisemiquavers   † semiquaver beam cancelled

zwei Hände

accorde

linke Hand

zulezt aufs leiseste

f. 40
see also
p. 105

★ ms: quavers

★ *also sketched on f. 47v (p. 199)*

188

2ter theil

thema

usw

[sic]

[3]

usw

f. 42

usw

usw

★ *minim stem cancelled*

*these series of crotchets lack dots in the ms.

f. 43
see also
p. 162

No 100 No 100

Mineur in
a moll D.c.

Mineur in
C moll d.c.

★ *the rests are all written as 𝄽*   † *these notes read a step lower in the ms.*

f. 44
see also
pp. 59–60

f. 45
see also
p. 47

[Handel, Fugue in G minor]

[sic]

★ *semiquaver beam cancelled*

usw

bis

bis

★ see note to the Quartet (?) for Wind Instruments and Piano, pp. 287—88.

f. 46

see also
pp. 46, 72,
157–58

Vari

f. 47

see also
pp. 158—59

Mineur zum Menuett in as

allegro

[continuous?]

nicht weit
ausgeführt

† allegro

★ *this crotchet was originally a quaver; it is followed by an extra quaver chord.*

† *also sketched on f. 40r (p. 188)*

f. 48

see also
pp. 39–40, 42

fuga und hernach mit tempo di minueto aufhören

in 8va l.H.

★ in the ms, the sharp appears to the left of the rest.

f. 49 see also pp. 41–42

side: wie das duett Concert auf zwei harm[onie] wo die second Harm[onie] meistens voraus blässt
u.s.w. auf die Art Klawier[—?] Konzert, überhaupt die bejden Hände mehr konzertieren lassen.

f. 50 see also pp. 72–73

★ semiquaver beam cancelled   † the direction of the stems follows the ms.

202

★ *the ms lacks the quaver beam and the ledger lines for the E.*

f. 51

see also
p. 163

★ *see also f. 100 (p. 238).*

★ *the dots may indicate that triplet semiquavers were intended.*

★ the flat appears to the right of the chord.

f. 54

[variant]

[piano studies?]

★ ms: an extra F''

f. 56   *see also pp. 169–71*

★ *perhaps to be read in the treble clef*   † *this passage can also be read*   ‡ *an illegible word?*

213

f. 57
see also
pp. 170–71

214

f. 58
see
pp. 13–14

f. 59
see also
pp. 22, 89, 174

★ *minim stem cancelled*

★ *demisemiquaver beam cancelled*

f. 62 f. 63

see
pp. 94, 96

★ *presumably the accompaniment is to be read one bar forward (or back).*

★ *an illegible word or abbreviation*

★ *semiquaver beam cancelled*

f. 67 see also pp. 161—62

★ an illegible word or abbreviation

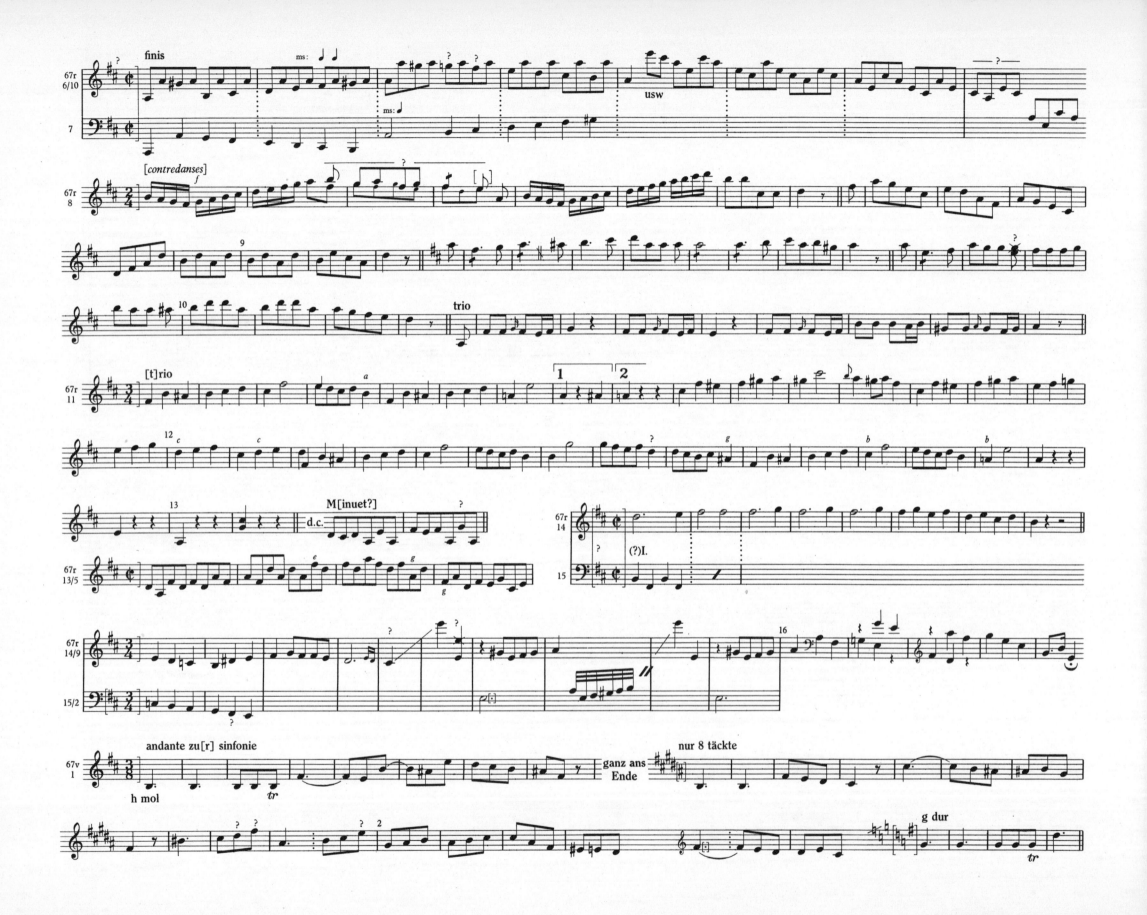

222

f. 69
see also
pp. 1, 3, 7

presto
aus as
ins a
8ven Sprünge

andante

fuga   fuga

wegen den Antworten in den Fugen einige Täge

f. 70   see also
pp. 175–76

★ ms: signature of two sharps

f. 71 *see also pp. 66, 169*

f. 72 *see also pp. 36, 70*

f. 73 *see also pp. 81, 83—84*

★ *the time signature appears below the third semiquaver group (?).*

225

ff. 74—80 *see also pp. 137—45, p. 69 (for f. 75), p. 91 (for ff. 75—76), and pp. 100—101 (for ff. 76—79)*

f. 81 *see pp. 39—40, 176*   **f. 82** *see also pp. 58, 89, 177*

f. 83 *see also pp. 8, 10—11*

Basso   fagot   corni   fagot   corn   fagot   corni   Basso

f dur ist besser dazu wegen dem f oben.

ff. 84—85 *see pp. 134—36*   **f. 86** *see also pp. 5—6*

f. 87 *see pp. 80—81*   **f. 88** *see also p. 89*

★ *an extra quaver rest in the ms.*

227

diese ganze Stelle ist gestohlen aus der Mozartschen Sinfonie in c wo das Andante in 68tel aus den (?)

★ *the natural appears to the left of the bar line.*

★ *a large* V[i] ?   † *it appears that the bracket originally began here.*

Allegro con brio

ganz staccato

beacoup

pp beacoup

f. 89

see also
pp. 45—46

mit der Hand geworfen.

★ possibly these figures are to be repeated.   † originally a quaver

230

[Mozart, 'Der Vogelfänger bin ich ja']

adagio

ff. 90—95   f. 96   f. 97

see pp. 110—25   see pp. 131—33,   see also
and note on p. 293   pp. 34, 54—55

★ these minims were all originally written as crotchets.   † the E♭ is repeated at the end of staff 7.

★ *many of the minims in this excerpt lack dots in the ms.*   † *semiquaver beam cancelled*

235

f. 99

see also
p. 133

★ *semiquaver beam cancelled*

f. 101
see pp. 18–19, 150

f. 102
see also pp. 19–20, 84

★ see also f. 50 (p. 204).   † ms: an extra accidental

238

f. 103   *see also pp. 15, 69, 102*

f. 104   *see also pp. 67–68, 82–83*

f. 105   *see pp. 65–66, 68, 83*   f. 106   *see pp. 61–62, 66*   ff. 107–108   *see p. 91–92*   f. 109   *see note on p. 294*

f. 110   *see also p. 12*

★ *there is an extra note in this scale.*   † *the mark appears to the right of the barline.*

f. 111 *see also p. 102*

f. 113 *see pp. 34–35, 38*

f. 114 *see also pp. 108–109*

f. 115 *see p. 109*

f. 116 *see also pp. 2–3, 7, 95*

f. 117 *see p. 156*

★ *i.e., another bass note—C?*

f. 119   *see also pp. 9, 11*
         39, 41–42, 77–79

f. 120
see also
p. 63

★ *semiquaver beam cancelled?*   † *ms: an extra bass clef*

f. 121

see also pp. 26, 28–31, 33

moderato   leztes allegro zu eine[m] quartett

ms:

f. 122 *see also pp. 27–32*

2 [illegible words]

[continuous?]

Allegretto

f. 123 *see also pp. 85–86*

mit liegendem Bass auf
die Art eines bären Tanzes

die haltende Noten im Bass verursachen guten Effect weil
der bass länger anhält, als in der höhe bej solchen Noten

usw

f. 124 *see also pp. 72, 98—99, 125*

f. 125 *see also p. 86*

★ *i.e., a third or a tenth above the bass?*

★ or 'ten'

245

dazu (?) eine umänderung einiger Stellen im Mozartischen C.[onzert?]

★ or '3ter'?

246

★ *this remark may refer to the end of the previous notation.*   † *presumably the sequence was to have been continued here.*

[torn] das tutti

usw

[obscure]

Cadenz

[blot]

es

hinan   hinan

um hier überraschung bejm Zuhörer zu bewirken muss
gleich nach einigen Täckten der schluss Triller vorkommen
und mit demselben in einen etwas entfernten Ton modulirt
werden und nach diesen [cut] nicht (?) aus (?)geführt werden

f. 126   *see also pp. 4, 72*

ms:

[contredanses]

linke Hand

[continuous?]

★ *minim stem cancelled*

248

f. 127
see also
pp. 48—49, 166

allegretto Rondo

f. 128
see also
pp. 166—68, 174

★ *semiquaver beam cancelled*   † *demisemiquaver beam cancelled*

f. 129
see pp.
177–82

f. 130
see also
pp. 90–91, 129

f. 131 see also p. 146

★see note on p. 295.

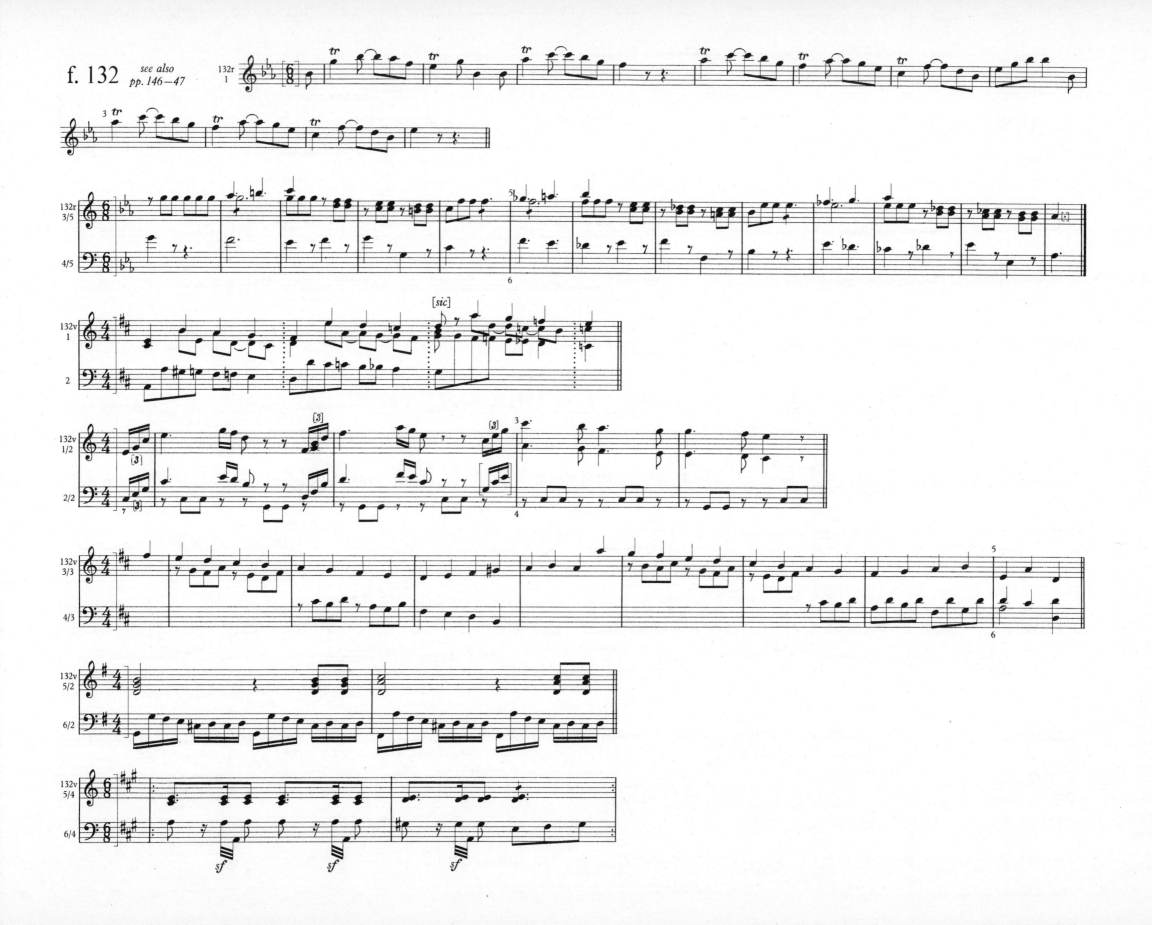

f. 132

see also pp. 146–47

f. 134
see also
pp. 49—50

ff. 135—137   f. 138
see pp. 73—78   see also
pp. 36—39

254

gehorig
zu ⊖

×
da Capo

D.C.

fp _____ pp

sobald jezt das Capo anfängt übernimmt die Klawierstimme den Gesang der Oboe, hernach
übernehmen alle blasende Stimmen den Hauptgesang, wobej das obige accompagnement N 100

f. 140

adagio

ms:

8va

257

★ *perhaps the first natural was added later, as a correction.*

f. 141
see also
pp. 159–60

★ *in the ms, the C appears before the flat.*   † *see notes on pp. 295 and 296.*   ‡ *in the ms, the rest appears at the left of the barline.*

[Mozart, Canon 'O du eselhafter Martin']

f. 142
see also
pp. 8—9

f. 143   see pp. 16—17, 24, 150—51   ff. 144—145   see pp. 150—55   f. 146   see pp. 23—24, 154—55

f. 147
see also
pp. 51—54

Andante

guten effect

Menuet

f. 148
see also pp. 45,
49, 51—54

[counterpoint exercises]

in 8va

Unisono

f. 149 *see also pp. 147, 156–57, 160*

f. 150 *see also pp. 126–27, 149*

★ *possibly arpeggiated G-major triads in the bass clef*　　† *minim stem cancelled*

262

f. 151

see also
pp. 148—49

[continuous?]

[variant]

usw

[contin-

263

★ *semiquaver beam cancelled.*

f. 153

see also
pp. 94, 165

★ *semiquaver beam cancelled*

f. 154 *see also*
pp. 73, 127–28

f. 155 *see also*
pp. 23, 58, 71

f. 156
see also
pp. 21–22

f. 158

see also pp. 83,
130, 167, 182

★ *or 'coda'?*

16/3: see p. 269

f. 159
see also
pp. 172—74

12/6

f. 160
see also
p. 64

[etc.]

[continuous?]

Andante

[continuous?]

tr   tr   usw   quintetto ★   corno 1mo
                                                                                          usw

[continuous?]

★ *see f. 161r, staffs 1—2 (p. 272).*

f. 161 *see also*
p. 104

Allegro†

Fagot

corno

★ *the chord and the rest appear to the left of the barline.*   † *for the quintet mentioned at f. 160v, staff 3? see p. 271.*

★ *semiquaver beam cancelled*   † *ms: an erroneous treble clef is inserted here.*   ‡ *this word may refer to the G-major item below, staffs 15—16 (p. 274).*

NOTES

THE notes include references to all previously published transcriptions, listed under the sources of publication (generally Nottebohm, *Zweite Beethoveniana*, and Shedlock, 'Beethoven's Sketch Books') in the order of their appearance there. The notes also provide a summary statement or discussion of the dates of the works or folios involved, and a listing of related sketches. The recent *Verzeichnis der Skizzen Beethovens* by Hans Schmidt has been of help for these listings; the editor has been able to supplement it in a number of cases. Notes for part 2 of the transcription (smaller sketches and miscellaneous notations, arranged by folios) also include information about the paper of the various folios, with reference to the Table of Paper-Types, Volume I, p. xxvi.

References to the manuscript are given by folio number, staff number, and bar number. Material on a brace of staffs is designated by the numbers of the staffs with a plus mark. Where no bar number appears, the reference is to be understood as encompassing the entire staff or brace. Thus 69^r 5/3f indicates a sketch, etc., beginning at bar 3 of staff 5 on f. 69 recto, and 139^v 1 + 2f indicates a sketch in piano score beginning with the first bar of staffs 1 and 2, braced, on f. 139 verso, and continuing past the end of those staffs. In counting bars, initial fractional bars are omitted, and no restitution is made in cases where obvious bar lines may have been left out in the manuscript.

ABBREVIATIONS

And.	*The Letters of Beethoven*, ed. Emily Anderson, 3 vols., London, 1961
B	Beethoven
B 28	Berlin Staatsbibliothek, Beethoven Autograph MS. 28 [S. 31]
GA	*Ludwig van Beethoven's Werke*, Leipzig, 1862–1949 (*Gesamtausgabe*)
GA Supplement	*Beethoven: Supplemente zur Gesamtausgabe*, ed. Willy Hess, Wiesbaden, 1959–
GdMf	Vienna, Gesellschaft der Musikfreunde
Hess	Willy Hess, *Verzeichnis der nicht in der Gesamtausgabe veröffentlichten Werke Ludwig van Beethovens*, Wiesbaden, 1957
HH	Augustus Hughes-Hughes, *Catalogue of Manuscript Music in the British Museum*, 3 vols., London, 1906–9
KH	Georg Kinsky and Hans Halm, *Das Werk Beethovens: Thematisch-Bibliographisches Verzeichnis*, Munich and Duisburg, 1955
Müller-Reuter	Theodor Müller-Reuter, *Lexikon der deutschen Konzertliteratur*, supplementary vol., Leipzig, 1921
N	Nottebohm; Gustav Nottebohm, *Zweite Beethoveniana*, Leipzig, 1887
NBA	*Beethoven: Werke*, Munich and Duisburg, 1961– (*Neue Beethoven-Ausgabe*)
S.	Hans Schmidt, *Verzeichnis der Skizzen Beethovens*, in *Beethoven-Jahrbuch*, vi (Jg. 1965/68), 1969, 7–128
Schiedermair	Ludwig Schiedermair, *Der junge Beethoven*, Bonn, 1925, 3rd edn., 1951
Sh	Shedlock; J. S. Shedlock, 'Beethoven's Sketch Books', *Musical Times*, xxxiii (1892), 331, 394, 461, 523, 589, 649 et seq.
sk, skk	sketch, sketches
ThF, ThR	*Thayer's Life of Beethoven*, ed. Elliot Forbes, Princeton, 1964, rev. edn., 1967; or ed. Hugo Riemann, Leipzig, 1907–11
TR	transcription, transcribes
WoO	*Werk ohne Opuszahl*, work without opus number (Kinsky-Halm)

Op. 1 Nos. 2 and 3 Piano Trios in G and C minor

N 21–8 (TR 69^r 5/3f, 69^v 5, 139^v 1 + 2f), 229; Sh 395–7 (TR 69^v 7f, 9 + 10, 11 + 12, 86^r 1/1f, 9/3f, 14/2f, 86^v 5 + 6/1f, 13/3f, 15 + 16/1f—which Sh related to WoO 28—116^v 1 + 2, 3 + 4/1f, 16/7f); *GA Supplement*, viii. 13 (the incomplete piano score of the G-major scherzo, f. 126).

Publ. May 1795. According to Ries, the trios Op. 1 were played for Haydn before his departure for London, i.e. before Jan. 1794; Thayer believed they were written in Bonn (ThF 164–5). But as N remarked, the skk are later (ff. 68–9 also contain fugue subjects presumably written for Albrechtsberger in 1794–5; f. 116 also contains skk for WoO 118, 1795) and these skk imply full-scale composing, not mere revision, as Thayer supposed. Ff. 69, 86, and 116 all contain late skk for one of the fast movements of the G-major Trio together with early skk for the C-minor; 69 also contains early skk for the largo of the G-major. On the other hand, f. 139 shows that the C-minor finale used an earlier theme, originally an andante for piano. N dated this sheet '1793 at the latest'(?).

p. 2 116^v 8/2f the material of this small sk refers to bar 304f, but its position seems to refer to the retransition.

p. 4 this incomplete piano score of the G-major scherzo may of course be later than the publication date.

p. 5 this draft in *alla breve* confirms Wegeler's report that the time signature of this movement was changed to 2/4 on the advice of the cellist Kraft (ThF 171).

p. 6 86^v 10 it seems that after writing staff 10, B wrote a variant aligned with it on 11/4f continuing to 12, then another variant (or insert) on 11/1–3—and perhaps another on staff 8.

p. 7 69^v 1f the naturals at the start of staff 2 seem to imply that staff 1 is in C minor. It is also possible that the page started with staff 2, with the naturals referring to something else, and that staff 1 was added later (see the sign at the beginning). 139^v 1 it is tempting to suppose that the term 'Rondo-mässig' was added when B returned to this andante theme and decided to employ it in the finale. 3 + 4/3 the direction 'Seite 1000 No 30' must refer to a lost page.

Other skk, for the G-major Trio: B 28 ff. 40 (TR in N 21, 23–4), 47 (TR in N 25), 49 (TR in N 22–3)—the latter skk together with more study fugues; GdMf 75 (contrapuntal studies; see Nottebohm, *B's Studien*, p. 202); for the C-minor Trio: B 28 f. 55 (TR in N 26). No skk are known for the Trio in E♭, Op. 1 No. 1.

Op. 5 Nos. 1 and 2 Sonatas for Violoncello and Piano in F and G minor

Sh 649–50 (TR 142^r 10/1f, 2/10 and 3/4f, 83^r 7/1f, 7/9f, 7/17f). Played by B with J. P. Duport (cf. ff. 57, 109) in Berlin in mid 1796. Publ. Feb. 1797.

p. 8 83^v 1f probably not a sk, but a late notation made in connection with the autograph of the F-major Sonata. The notation occurs in the midst of skk for the G-minor Sonata, showing that the G-minor was composed later, as implied by the order of publication.

p. 9 f. 142$^{r, v}$ several of these very hasty skk are related thematically to the F-major Sonata, others are not, but it may be assumed that all belong to an early stage of its composition. The reading is tentative. 142^r 10 this sk is unclear; the theme may not have reached its final form. 119^v 5 the scattered but precise and boldly written notations for Op. 5 Nos. 1 and 2 on f. 119^v also look less like skk than notes made in connection with the autograph, or even the proof.

pp. 10–11 the order of the drafts on 83^v 7f, 83^r 9 + 10f, and 83^v 5/5f is uncertain. B was recasting a passage from the exposition for use in the recapitulation.

p. 11 83^r 9 + 10 the intent of the diagonal barline and the inscription is not clear. 119^v 7 see note to 119^v 5, above.

Other skk: B 28 ff. 13 (both sonatas), 14 (F major).

Op. 6 Sonata in D for Piano, Four Hands

Publ. Oct. 1797. Other D-major skk on the same bifolium (110^r 1 + 2f, 111^r 3/1f, 4 + 5/1f) may have been intended for the sonata also.

p. 12 110^v 2 B's intention is not clear; the solution here is tentative. *Besser nur durchaus*: better just straight through, i.e., omitting the repeat (as is done in the final version).

Op. 7 Piano Sonata in E♭

N 508–12 (TR 58^v 6f, 58^r 1/9f, 6/5f, 58^v 4 + 5/1f); Sh 462 (TR 58^r 4/9f, 5/1f, 2/1f, 10/4f, 58^v 10/1f).

Publ. Oct. 1797. Sketched on a bifolium (ff. 58–9) which also contains a notation for WoO 71, composed between Sept. 1796 and Apr. 1797. It also has a sk for the trio of the minuet of the Sonata in D, Op. 10 No. 3, in the key of A♭ but evidently notated in three flats; the piece may well have been first conceived for Op. 7.

With this interesting set of skk, the order of writing is hard to determine, especially on f. 58^r. The continuity is uncertain at several points, notably at 58^r 5/19. On internal evidence, 58^v was written first.

Another sk, for the finale: B 28 f. 27, with skk for Op. 10 No. 1.

Op. 8 Serenade for String Trio

Publ. Oct. 1797.

p. 15 103ᵛ 11 the beginning of this sk has been crowded in later. 10/3*f* tentatively identified as a sk for the adagio only by its context; there is no thematic connection. (For a somewhat similar sk, see f. 56ᵛ.)

Op. 9 No. 1 String Trio in G

N 515 (TR 143ʳ 1/1*f*); facs. and TR of a second trio for the scherzo in A. Schmitz, *B : Unbekannte Skizzen.*

Publ. July 1798.

pp. 16–17 the movement drafted on f. 143ʳ is probably an early idea for the finale of this trio, or even the scherzo, though N identified it merely as a 'rondo-like work' for cello and piano. It appears on the same page as a brief sk for the slow movement of the trio and skk for Op. 11, which was composed around the same time; also the first and second subjects in the draft bear some relation to those ultimately used in the trio, and the words 'viola'(?) and 'violoncello' appear at staffs 7 and 10, where the texture is consonant with that of a string trio. B's note at the end indicates that this short movement was to have been extended or followed by an adagio.

The draft is of interest in that it presents a sonata-form movement with a fugato theme which acquires new countersubjects at the recapitulation. Other movements of this type appear in Op. 10 No. 2, Op. 18 No. 4, and Op. 21.

p. 17 143ᵛ 6/13 the remark 'a tre theme' may refer to the passage below, 7/8.

Other skk, for the first movement: B 28 f. 42, similar to f. 66ʳ; for the adagio and movements from the other trios: a sheet in private possession (S. 367; No. 249 in Albrecht's *Census of Autograph Music in American Libraries*); for the definitive version of the finale, etc.: B 28 f. 41 (TR in N 43).

Op. 10 No. 2 Piano Sonata in F

N 34–5 (TR 101ʳ 1*f*, 5/2*f*, 101ᵛ 1/9*f*); Sh 462 (TR 101ʳ 1/1*f*, 10/12*f*, 101ᵛ 1/1*f*, 3/1*f*, 4/1*f*).

The sonatas Op. 10 were probably composed (in order) directly after Op. 7, 1796–7. Publication was announced in July 1798.

Inscriptions referring to the sonatas Op. 10: 'Zu den neuen Sonaten ganze kurze Menuetten. Zu der aus dem C moll bleibt das presto [WoO 52?] weg' (N 32: on f. 82ʳ, with skk for WoO 53 and Op. 16, Apr. 1797); 'Die Menuetten zu den Sonaten inskünftige nicht länger als von höch[stens] 16 bis 24 T.—' (N 35: on f. 102ʳ, with skk for Op. 10 No. 3, etc.).

p. 18 the meaning of the referral marks is clear except for the 'oder' marks at 101ʳ 7 and 4/5; the latter may refer to the sk following.

p. 19 101ᵛ 1/9*f* cf. the Allegretto in C minor, WoO 53 (see p. 84), which was composed in connection with the sonatas Op. 10.

Op. 10 No. 3 Piano Sonata in D

N 35–40 (TR 102ᵛ 1*f*, 5+6*f*, 156ᵛ 5*f*, 157ʳ 6/6*f*, 156ᵛ 3/10*f* and 8+9/3*f*, 1+2/3*f*, 157ʳ 4+5/1*f*); Sh 463 (TR 102ᵛ 9/5*f*, 157ᵛ 9/12*f*, 156ᵛ 9/6*f*, 12/1, 157ʳ 4+5/1*f*, 59ᵛ 1/1*f*).

For the date and inscriptions referring to the sonatas Op. 10, see note above. D-major and B-minor skk on f. 156ʳ may refer to this sonata.

p. 19 the notes at 102ᵛ 9/5*f* are in a different ink, also used for the ' × ' at 4/2 and the revisions on 8/4*f*.

p. 22 the trio sk, evidently in the key of A♭ within a signature of three flats, appears on a bifolium with skk for Op. 7, 1796–7. It may well have been first conceived for Op. 7.

Other skk: B 28 ff. 30, 44 (TR in N 38), 45 (TR in N 37). Skk for Op. 10 No. 1 appear in B 28 ff. 7, 24, 27–9 (TR in N 29–34).

Op. 11 Trio for Clarinet, Violoncello, and Piano

N 516 (TR 146ᵛ 1/11*f*, 143ʳ 16/1*f*, 146ᵛ 13/1*f*; N's discussion of the first sk is in error).

Publ. Oct. 1798. The finale (which is not sketched) uses a theme from Weigl's *L'amor molinaro*, which opened Oct. 1797.

p. 24 146ᵛ 8*f* this draft runs from the back page of the gathering ff. 143–6 to the front. The reading is highly conjectural at several points.

Op. 13 Piano Sonata in C minor ('Pathétique')

N 42–3 (TR 66ʳ 3/7*f*).

Publ. autumn 1799, but probably written some time earlier; on two similar sheets, f. 66 and B 28 f. 41, the rondo is sketched together with Op. 9, which was publ. July 1798. The Sonata Movement in C minor (i), sketched in 1797–8, may also have been intended for Op. 13.

As N observed, the chords in the skk suggest that at one time the piece was conceived for violin.

p. 25 66ʳ 7–10 in this context, the strong upward motion of these skk irresistibly recalls the first movement of Op. 13; but the identification is very tentative.

Another sk: B 28 f. 41 (TR in N 42), similar to f. 66ʳ.

Op. 14 No. 1 Piano Sonata in E

N 45-59 (TR [allegro] 65ᵛ 9/5f, 121ʳ 5f, 122ᵛ 9f, 8/1f, 14f, 17f, 121ᵛ 1f, [allegretto] 122ʳ 6/1f, 7f, 16 + 17/10f, [rondo] 122ʳ 10 + 11f, 16/3f, 121ᵛ 16/11f); Sh 464 (TR 65ᵛ 13 + 14/12f, 16/3f, 18/5f, 121ᵛ 8/1f).

These skk, which are among the most extensive in the miscellany, appear on two bifolia of identical paper (type 18). Since on f. 65 sonata skk follow late skk for the finale of Op. 19, N dated the sonata in 1795. The delay in publication—until Dec. 1799—might be explained by B's wish to publish larger, more impressive sonatas first (Op. 7, 10, 13). However, Riemann disputed the 1795 date on internal evidence (see note to Op. 19).

As N observed, the skk show that all three movements were composed simultaneously, a fact of interest in view of their thematic interrelations. N's cryptic suggestion (N 47) that the sonata was originally conceived for string quartet may derive from the inscription on 121ʳ 14, 'leztes allegro zu einem quartett', which does not, however, refer to a sonata sk (see p. 243).

The skk illustrate well the difficulty of determining the sequence of writing on crowded B sk pages. A suggested order of writing is 65ᵛ, 121ʳ, 122ʳ, 122ᵛ, 121ᵛ, with the following sonata skk inserted later, when the pages were loosely filled: 65ᵛ 16-18, 121ʳ 12 + 13/9f, 14 + 15/4f, 16 + 17/1f, 122ʳ 3/1f, 3/5f, 121ᵛ 4/4f, 8. According to this interpretation, the skk in E major, 2/4 time, on 121ʳ 1 + 2 and 122ʳ 5 (p. 31) could be early ideas for a finale, and 122ʳ 10 + 11f (p. 32) would probably be the first draft for the finale with its present themes.

p. 25 65ᵛ 9 + 10/5f for the second note of the fugato, N's reading was E, but F is also possible, and more orthodox.

p. 27 the relationship between the drafts on 122ᵛ 9f and 2/6f is unclear. They are almost identical except for the gaps in 2/6f. This may have been written later.

p. 28 122ᵛ 8 the words 'bis nach dem ×' appear to have been added later. There is no '×' to be found.

p. 29 121ʳ 12 + 13/9f the last bars of this sk are widely separated from the rest.

p. 31 121ᵛ 13 the reading is tentative. 121ʳ 1/15 Dr. Weise suggests that the words may be 'in gis mo'.

p. 33 121ᵛ 17/18 the 'Vi:' is puzzling; it appears to have been written directly after 17/18, yet it would not have been necessary if 17/19 had not already been present.

Other skk: B 28 f. 31 (TR in N 45-6), followed by skk for Op. 12 No. 2; a cut sheet in private possession (copy in the Hertzmann Collection, Columbia

University); a cut sheet at the Royal Musical Academy, Stockholm (S. 375; see *Svensk Tidskrift f. Musikforskning*, iii [1921], 83-5, with facs.). No skk have been found for the Sonata in G, Op. 14 No. 2.

Op. 15 Piano Concerto in C

N 64-8 (TR 113ʳ 1f, 113ᵛ 1/6f); Sh 524-5 (TR 97ᵛ 1/1f, 72ᵛ 12, 13/1f, 113ᵛ 1 + 2/6f).

The autographs of B's first concertos, Op. 19 and Op. 15, are undated, and there are still unsolved problems about their history. B tells us that Op. 15 is the later (And. 48). There are references to performances of B concertos in Mar. and Dec. 1795 (the keys are not mentioned); then both works are reported to have been played in Oct. 1798. As Sh observed, skk for Op. 15 on ff. 72 and 97 point to 1795, since these folios also have skk for WoO 8 and Op. 19. KH concludes that Op. 15 was drafted in 1795-6 and completed in 1798.

Of the many pianistic fragments in C major on ff. 72 and 138, only a few refer to themes in the Allegro con brio of Op. 15, but it may be assumed that all were intended for that movement, probably for the cadenza. F. 138ʳ has concordances with Op. 15 cadenza skk on B 28 f. 30 (TR in N 67-8). F. 138ᵛ is one of the more cryptic pages in the miscellany: besides the putative cadenza skk on staffs 6-16, 3-5 may refer to the largo (note the theme at the end) and 8/10 etc., marked 'le dernier allegro', may refer to the finale. The case is far from clear, but more likely than not all this material refers to Op. 15. Again, the skk on 113ᵛ 9 + 10f and 16 can be associated with the concerto only tentatively.

p. 35 113ʳ 11/6 this little variant may refer to 10/7, as suggested by the alignment, or 10/10, where an '×' seems to be written below the staff (but 11/6 proposes no emendment to 10/10). 113ʳ 11/7 possibly continuous from the previous draft.

p. 36 72ᵛ 12 the word is 'Anfang' with a flourish on the 'f', according to Dr. Weise. 138ʳ 3 *stumpf*: blunt(?).

p. 37 138ʳ 10 *gegen B[ewegung]*: contrary motion.

p. 38 113ᵛ 1 a signature of four flats for the key of D♭ is not uncommon with B: see f. 64ʳ 1 + 2 and A. Schmitz, *B: Unbekannte Skizzen*, p. 22.

Other skk, for a first-movement cadenza: B 28 f. 30 (TR in N 67-8), with skk for Op. 10 No. 3, 1796-8; for the largo(?): GdMf 62 [S. 292]; for the finale: Beethovenhaus Bodmer 63 (S. 110; see *Zeitschrift für Musikwissenschaft*, xvii [1935], 546); a sheet described by Th. v. Frimmel, *L. v. Beethoven*, 6th edn., 1922, pp. 86-7. See also notes to the Song in C (i) and f. 103.

Op. 16 Quintet for Wind Instruments and Piano

N 513-14 (TR 81ʳ 2f, 49ʳ 7/1f); Sh 651 (TR 81ʳ 2/1f, 3/10f, 1/7f, 6/6f, 49ʳ 7/1f).

Performed Apr. 1797. Of the sk folios, 48-9 and 81 are of paper-type 10c, which dates from 1796, and although 119 looks older, the Op. 16 skk were obviously added later than the other contents. Since the bifolium 48-9 has definite skk for Op. 16, several less definite skk on it may also be tentatively associated with the work: three first-movement skk on 48ʳ (p. 39), three andante sk on 48ᵛ (p. 40), two rondo skk on 49ᵛ, and a rondo cadenza sk on 48ᵛ (p. 42). For the tradition that B himself improvised during performances of Op. 16, see ThF 197, 350. The skk do not support KH's suggestion that the first movement was completed 'several years earlier (1794?)'.

p. 42 48ʳ 1 B writes an 'ideal' high G; his piano did not have this note.

Other skk, for the introduction: B 28 f. 14, on a bifolium with skk for Op. 5, 1796.

Op. 18 No. 5 String Quartet in A

Sh 650 (TR 152ʳ 5/1f [erroneous], 6/1, 11/4f).

Composed 1799.

Almost the whole of f. 152ʳ was marked with braces and barlines (and even double bars, with repeat marks) for a quartet score, but this was soon abandoned. The sheet must have been rejected from a rough working autograph of the andante of the quartet, quite possibly from the mutilated sketchbook Berlin Aut. 19e [S. 29], which contains the same paper, and includes skk for other of the Op. 18 quartets. 'Var 5' and the preceding *minore* do not figure in the final version, but the superimposed skk on staffs 5-7 became var. 3. Thereafter the page was crammed with late finale skk. A-major skk on the verso are conceivably early ideas for the finale.

Other skk: Berlin, Gr. 2, ff. 54-5, 65-9, 74 (TR in N 489-90).

Op. 19 Piano Concerto in B♭

N 66 (TR 46ʳ 1+2/4f), 69-73 (TR 64ᵛ 11/1f, 147ᵛ 12/*end*-13, 147ᵛ 1, 148ᵛ 8/1f, 8/*end*, 14+15/1f, 97ʳ 1+2/1f); Sh 523-4 (TR 64ᵛ 11/1f, 15/5f, 4/1f [erroneous], 148ʳ 14/1f, 148ᵛ 14/*end*, 89ᵛ 3+4f, 89ʳ 9+10/5f, 3+4/5f, 97ʳ 5/1, 9/1); the score on f. 89ʳ is mentioned by Müller-Reuter, p. 63.

The autographs of B's first concertos, Op. 19 and 15, are undated, and there are still unsolved problems about their history. B tells us that Op. 19 was the earlier (And. 48). There are references to performances of B concertos in Mar. and Dec. 1795 (the keys are not mentioned); then both works are reported to have been played in Oct. 1798. With Op. 19, the situation is complicated by evidence of a revision in the sketchbook Gr. 1, 1798-9 (N 479-81; see also the unpubl. Bonn dissertation by Erna Szabo, 1953). N established that the concerto played in Mar. 1795 was Op. 19, on the evidence of the bifolium ff. 147-8, which contains canonic exercises presumably written for Albrechtsberger before early 1795, and skk for all three movements of Op. 19. N argued that all the movements must have been written together in time for the Mar. performance.

This led N to take other positions of some importance: (1) an autograph exists for a Rondo in B♭ for Piano and (the same) Orchestra, WoO 6, a work that is hard to account for except as an early finale for Op. 19. Mandyczewski built a good case for this on internal evidence (*Sammelbände der internationalen Musikgesellschaft*, i [1899-1900], 295-306), but N had been obliged to deny it. (2) Since skk for the Sonata in E, Op. 14 No. 1, and the Violin Sonata in A, Op. 12 No. 2, are contemporary with concerto skk, N placed these works too in 1795, though they were not published until 1799. Riemann disputed this on internal evidence, postulating that the skk on ff. 147-8 were added to an old sheet at the point of revision in 1798 (ThR, ii. 96). In point of fact, the single sk on ff. 147-8 for the first movement refers to a passage (development, bar 248f) for which there are actually two early score fragments in existence: Paris Conservatoire 61 (Hess 14: see *B-Jahrbuch*, v [1966], 84 and *GA Supplement*, iii. 3) and Beethovenhaus 121 (ibid. 70-1). Hess says the latter is similar in appearance to the autograph of WoO 6 (ibid. 76). The London sk transmits a form in between that of the Bonn fragment and the final version. It therefore appears that the skk on 147-8 refer to a revision of the concerto at a point when B discarded the Bonn page and the WoO 6 autograph, revised the first movement (and also the second?), and composed the new finale.

This could have been as early as late 1795, in time for the Dec. performance. Wegeler reports of the première in March that the finale was written two days before (ThF 173-4); B may well have been dissatisfied with his hurried original production. In the editor's opinion, the 1798 date does not accord with the appearance of the numerous sk pages. The form of the treble clef, the form of the brace bracket, and B's whim of sketching without barlines, all point to the earlier period.

p. 45 unlike the Bonn fragment, the score fragment on f. 89 was not discarded from an early autograph; it breaks off after four bars without filling the page. It must preserve part of a rejected revision. Of the many pianistic fragments added to this folio, most (though not all) appear to be in B♭ major and some refer to the first theme of the concerto. All the B♭ fragments are here interpreted as studies for a cadenza. On f. 46ʳ some of the identical fragments are repeated.

p. 46 89^r 9 + 10/5f Sh read this in the key of C and related it to Op. 15.

pp. 48–9 It is hard to avoid the conclusion that the inscription on f. 127^v, 'Concerto in B dur adagio in d dur', refers to the draft overleaf, and that the concerto was Op. 19—there can hardly have been another piano concerto in B♭ in 1795, which is the date indicated for 127 by early skk for the unfinished Symphony in C (q.v.). It therefore appears that at one time Op. 19 was going to have (or actually had) a slow movement in D, not E♭. This full-scale draft for a piano concerto adagio may be compared with a similar item from Bonn, pp. 127–8.

p. 49 B sketched much of Op. 19, and other works of the same time, without barlines.

p. 50 the skk on f. 134$^{r, v}$ are often uncertain as to continuity. 64^v 1 + 2 these skk appear on a sheet with rondo skk; they may refer to the adagio, though there is no thematic connection.

p. 51f skk for the rondo are among the most extensive in the miscellany. They are arranged here in three 'phases' according to the different sheets or bifolia, which are of different paper types. The skk on ff. 64–5 are clearly the latest, though N took them to be early on account of the rhythmic form of the main theme; this evidently caused B several changes of mind.

Early Phase. The skk are thoroughly confused on the pages, but it is possible to associate most of them with definite sections of the movement.

p. 52 147^v 6 the first two bars of this sk, and its position, suggest that it goes with the line above; but the ending is obscure.

p. 54 Intermediate Phase 97^r 1 + 2f the interpretation of the signs and referral marks in this draft is tentative.

Other skk: Berlin, Gr. 1, ff. 19–21 (facs. of 21^v in *Die Musik*, xxiii [1930], opp. p. 16); Paris 70 [S. 223].

Op. 37 Piano Concerto in C minor

Sh 525 (TR all three skk); W. Osthoff, *B: Klavierkonzert C-moll* (*Meisterwerke der Musik*, ii, 1965: facs. and TR of the skk on f. 82^r).

The concerto was not played till 1803, at a famous concert with the first two symphonies and *Christus am Oelberge*, but the autograph is dated 1800 and the early skk on f. 82 appear on a bifolium with skk for Op. 16, which was played in Apr. 1797, and the sk on f. 155—for an idea ultimately used in the cadenza—precedes skk for Op. 10 No. 3, which was publ. July 1799.

Another sk: for a cadenza, Beethovenhaus Bodmer 71 [S. 118] (see *NBA*, vii [vii], p. VIII).

Op. 46 Adelaide ('Einsam wandelt dein Freund')

N 536–9 (TR 44^r 1f).

Composed 1795.

Other skk: Vienna GdMf 35 (S. 264; TR in N 536 and Thayer, *Verzeichnis*, No. 43); GdMf 75 (contrapuntal studies), p. 202 (N 229); Paris 40 (S. 193; overleaf from more studies); Beethovenhaus Bodmer 62 (S. 109; partial facs. in Seyfried, *B's Studien*, p. 353). Cf. also Berlin Artaria 149 (TR in N 538) and Beethovenhaus 99. In *B's Studien*, p. 230, N transcribed excerpts from GdMf 75 and elsewhere.

Op. 49 No. 1 Sonatina in G minor for Piano

N 44.

Composed 1797? F. 66, first used to begin a fair copy, was later used to sketch Op. 9, publ. July 1798, and Op. 13. This provides a *terminus ante quem* for the sonatina, but it is impossible to say how much time lapsed between the fair copy and the skk.

Op. 49 No. 2 Sonatina in G for Piano

Nottebohm, *Beethoveniana*, p. 2 (TR 106^r 4/1f, 106^v 1f, 8/5f, 11/3f); Sh 461–2 (TR 106^r 4/1f, 5/5f, 6/4f, 7/2f, 106^v 1/1f, 3/1f).

Composed 1796, or possibly later: skk appear at the end of a series of pages containing Op. 65, 71, WoO 43b, and 44a, all dating from 1796.

p. 61 106^r 11–14/1 are written in soft red pencil or crayon, which is smeared and indistinct.

Op. 52 No. 2 Feuerfarb' ('Ich weiss eine Farbe')

HH, ii. 573; *GA Supplement*, v. 85, where the entire fragmentary autograph is transcribed.

The song in its original version (Hess 144; ibid. 10f) dates from 1792, and Hess calls the present fragment a 'first attempt' at the revised version, ultimately publ. 1805. A sk for the revision in B 28 f. 56, probably dating from 1793 (TR in N 518), can unfortunately not be compared with the London fragment since it concerns only the postlude, missing in London. The fragment could date from 1793 or a few years later.

Op. 52 No. 3 Das Liedchen von der Ruhe ('Im Arm der Liebe')

N 561 (TR 52^v 1/1f: 'um 1790'); Sh 591 (TR 52^v 1 + 2f, 15/1f).

N's 'um 1790' has been taken too literally by Schiedermair (p. 216) and ThF (p. 130); N would seem to have picked this date mainly to stress the length of time between the composition of this song and its publication in

1805. Handwriting and paper point to the early Vienna period; similar paper was used in 1795 (ff. 89–95). In that year B wrote a canon (his first known?) on the beginning words of the poem (WoO 159; cf. WoO 119).

For other instances of B sketching a song in two different metres, see the Songs in C (i) and (iii), and WoO 116.

Op. 65 'Ah! perfido', Scena and Aria for Soprano

Nottebohm, *Beethoveniana*, p. 1.

Composed 1796, but possibly sketched earlier.

The reading of the faded pencil skk is often uncertain, but they do seem to reveal some faulty Italian declamation; cf. N 539 and *B's Studien*, p. 207f.

Other skk: B 28 f. 43.

Op. 66 Variations on Mozart's 'Ein Mädchen oder Weibchen' for Violoncello and Piano

Publ. Sept. 1798. The skk are overleaf from the score of the unfinished Symphony in C, which was sketched in 1795–6. The variations were probably composed in 1796, the year of B's concerts with the cellist J. P. Duport. Another sheet with skk for the symphony (f. 158) bears traces of another set of Mozart variations for cello: see p. 182.

Op. 71 Sextet for Wind Instruments

Nottebohm, *Beethoveniana*, p. 1; N 40 (TR 103^r 3/1f).

Composed 1796? the copy of the minuet on f. 105 is followed by skk for Op. 65 (1796, or even earlier), but the finale skk on 103^r appear with Op. 10 Nos. 2 and 3, which were probably sketched somewhat later. And KH cautiously observes that the first two movements of the sextet may have been composed even earlier than 1796.

The minuet autograph differs in several details from the version ultimately published in 1810. In this MS. B has sometimes erased by smudging the ink out.

Op. 75 No. 3 Flohlied ('Es war einmal ein König')

H. Boettcher, *B als Liedkomponist*, Appendix.

Publ. 1810.

Overleaf from skk for WoO 67, 1791–2; other skk from this period appear on B 28 f. 1 (TR in N 563). Goethe's poem was publ. in 1790 (*Faust. Ein Fragment*). Beethovenhaus 114 [S. 88] has further skk from the early Vienna years (not 'gegen 1800', as N and Schmitz have it: facs. and TR in A. Schmitz, *B: Unbekannte Skizzen*; see also N 563).

WoO 6 Rondo in B♮ for Piano and Orchestra

N 70 (TR 75^v 12 + 13); see *GA Supplement*, iii. 73.

The skk, added to the autograph of the Bonn Romance in E minor, appear to date from Bonn also. But the rondo itself almost certainly figured as the original finale of Op. 19 (q.v.), which Wegeler says was written two days before the première in Mar. 1795. The andante episode, to which these skk refer, might have been an earlier piece hurriedly incorporated. Hess also suggests that this andante may have been considered for the slow movement of Op. 19 (loc. cit.).

WoO 8 Twelve Allemandes for Orchestra

Sh 525 (TR 72^r 1/1f).

Played at the Redoutensaal in Nov. 1795.

p. 70 it is hard to relate the inscription at the bottom of f. 72^r to this coda. 72^r 11/9f the original version is shown with upward stems.

Other skk: Beethovenhaus Bodmer 26/74 [S. 181].

WoO 11 Seven Ländler

N 40 (TR 155^r 8/6f).

Publ. early in 1799, but the skk are followed by skk for Op. 10 No. 3, publ. July 1798.

Of the dozen-odd dances sketched on f. 155, only one appears in WoO 11, but since all of them are in D major, the key of all the WoO 11 dances, they are evidently specific studies for this set rather than a series of random dances from which B made a selection later (cf. WoO 14 and the Allemandes and Contredanses, pp. 98–9). Even simple dances, it appears, sometimes cost B appreciable labour.

p. 71 it is of course not always certain which 8-bar periods belong together. 155^r 5/9 B's corrections are obscure. It is tentatively suggested that first he wrote 5/9 without the '3' mark or the last two quavers, followed by 5/10, 6/1, and 6/2; next cancelled 5/10 and corrected with the '×' mark leading to 6/11; and finally added the '3' mark and quavers to 5/9 and squeezed in 5/11–14 (with an erroneous '3' for '2' at 5/12). 155^r 7/1f, 7/3f, 8/1f the relation of these skk to one another is uncertain.

WoO 13 Twelve Allemandes for Orchestra

Publ. in *GA Supplement*, viii. 32–9.

Whatever may be the date of the collection as a whole (see KH), the trio to No. 10 is much earlier: f. 124 dates from Bonn, and contains skk for a large unfinished or lost set of dances with coda (see Allemandes and Contre-danses, pp. 98–9). F. 46 (Nos. 9 and 12) dates from 1795 or later. The trio to No. 8 may be derived from a dance on f. 54ʳ 1 + 2 (see p. 209).

WoO 14 Twelve Contredanses for Orchestra

N 229, 564; Sh 397 (TR 126ᵛ 6/1f).

As the only set of contredanses published by B (in 1802), this drew on material ranging over many years. Skk for some of the dances have been found in a sketchbook of 1802 [S. 263], whereas skk for Nos. 8 and 12 appear on the Bonn folios 50 and 154. F. 126 (Nos. 3 and 4) also contains the piano score of Op. 1 No. 2, publ. 1795 (though the piano score and/or the contre-danse skk could be later). The other four contredanse skk on this folio may also have been planned for WoO 14.

pp. 72–3 50ᵛ 1, etc. the material of No. 8 is sketched as though for a coda.

WoO 32 Duo for Viola and Violoncello 'mit zwei obligaten Augengläsern'

HH, iii. 180; publ. in *GA Supplement*, vi. 7–17.

The largest and most important autograph in the miscellany. Assumed to have been written for Nikolaus von Zmeskall, B's close friend from the earliest Vienna days, to whom B remarked in a letter of 1798: 'Je vous suis bien obligé pour votre faiblesse de vos yeux' (And. 30; Miss Anderson's suggestion that the duet was included in this letter is unlikely, as will appear). Ff. 135–7 contain the first movement, much corrected but com-plete, and the second movement, broken off after a few bars. The minuet and trio, again complete, appear on a sheet of different paper, f. 119, which was later used for (1) a sk for the first movement (2) a sk for a C-minor scherzo for viola and violoncello, 119ʳ 15 (3) skk for Op. 16, performed Apr. 1797, and (4) skk or notations for the autograph of Op. 5, publ. Feb. 1797. The simplest construction to put on this evidence is that the minuet and trio was written first (possibly some time earlier than the other move-ments); that when B came to write the first movement he reviewed the minuet and decided against it, and so used the autograph to sketch the first movement and a new scherzo (as well as other works which can be dated in 1796 or early 1797); and that in any case he soon abandoned the duo al-together, leaving the slow movement unfinished.

An attempt has been made to supply readings for the cancellations and corrections in the first movement, but many are hardly legible. See Hess's discussion in *GA Supplement*, vi. 151–2.

p. 78 137ᵛ 1/1 a decorated version (added later?) has been cancelled. 119ʳ 1

282

as the top of this folio is badly worn, bars 5–6, 8, and 11–12 are not fully legible, but the reading can be supplied safely from the musical context.

p. 79 119ʳ 15/16 'c. p.' presumably stands for 'contrapunkt'.

WoO 43a Sonatina in C minor for Mandoline and Piano

Publ. in *GA*, xxv. 344–5; facs. of the autograph in *A reference Catalogue of British and foreign Autographs and Manuscripts*, ed. H. S. Wyndham, viii: *Beethoven*, by J. S. Shedlock, London, 1899.

This and the following three works were written in 1796 for Countess Josephine Clary, a singer and mandoline player, who married Count von Clam-Gallas in 1797. Copies of WoO 43b, 44a, and 44b were found in the Clam-Gallas family archive. See A. Buchner, 'Bs Kompositionen für Mandoline', *B-Jahrbuch*, iii (1959), 38–50.

p. 80 durchaus: straight through (without repeats).

p. 81 the interpretation of the ending as a coda follows the *GA*.

Other skk: B 28 f. 43, inscribed 'pour la Madmoiselle la Comtesse de Clari' (TR in N 221).

WoO 43b Adagio in E♮ for Mandoline and Piano

Two versions publ. in *GA Supplement*, ix. 34–40.

p. 82 B began sketching f. 104ʳ on the left-hand side: 104ʳ 4/1–4, 5/1–7, 6, 7/1–8. Then he used space at the right to enter the main draft (all at the same time?). The bottom of the page was left for variants.

Another sk: B 28 f. 43.

WoO 44a Sonatina in C for Mandoline and Piano

Publ. in *GA Supplement*, ix. 40–4. This rondo was probably meant to com-plete WoO 43a.

Other skk: B 28 f. 43 (TR in N 221).

WoO 44b Andante and Variations in D for Mandoline and Piano

Publ. in *GA Supplement*, ix. 44–50.

WoO 53 Allegretto in C minor for Piano (Hess 66)

Publ. in *GA*, xxv. 357–9; an earlier version (Hess 66) in *GA Supplement*, ix. 17–19.

Composed in connection with the sonatas Op. 10, probably in 1797; there are thematic similarities with Op. 10 No. 2 and with skk for Op. 14 No. 1: see p. 30 (KH 500). The skk refer to the earlier version (Hess 66).

p. 84 the inscription states alternatives for handling the scherzo section in the *da capo*: with this [new] sequence(?), or straight through (no repeats).

Other skk: B 28 ff. 27–9, with Op. 7 (publ. Oct. 1797) and Op. 10 No. 1.

WoO 65 Variations on 'Venni amore' by Righini, for Piano

Composed 1790, played by B at Aschaffenburg-am-Main in 1791, and publ. at Mannheim in 1791, though no copy of the edition has survived. Republished in 1801 'in a new, apparently heavily revised version', according to KH (p. 512). The Bonn sheets ff. 123 and 125, which constitute our only certain trace of the original version, were first noticed by J. V. Cockshoot, *The Fugue in B's Piano Music*, 1959, pp. 146–9 (TR the whole of var. '4' on 123ᵛ).

Against the common assumption, W. Kolneder has argued that the 1791 and 1802 versions were identical ('Evolutionismus und Schaffenschronologie: zu Bs Righini-Variationen', *Studien zur Musikgeschichte des Rheinlandes*, ii [1962], 119–32). His bibliographical argument is faulty, but the correspondences between the Bonn sheets and the 1802 version support his claim for at least some variations; and there is little reason to suspect 'heavy revision' in any of them.

F. 123ᵛ is described by Cockshoot as a page of skk in an advanced form; or else it may be part (page 2) of a discarded 'working autograph'—discarded, perhaps, when B decided to alter the order of the variations. Vars. 7, 6, 5, and 4 appear here numbered 4, 5, 6, 7. Such a MS. might have been begun before the work was fully planned, and so it is not too surprising to find skk for eight variations in an early state overleaf. B's (later?) inscription 'orgel Variationen' is surprising, though he is indeed known to have improvised variations on the organ in 1790 or 1791 (ThF 100).

p. 85 123ᵛ 1 + 2/9–13 evidently these bars should have been cancelled. 5 + 6/1–8 originally continuous quavers ending with the crochet and rest in 5 + 6/8. This was changed to incorporate a halt in 5/2, which necessitated a shift in the barlines and a new cadence—5 + 6/8 was cancelled and a rest inserted in 5 + 6/7. The old barlines should have been cancelled. 7 + 8/7*f* the original version is not clear.

WoO 67 Variations on a Theme by Count Waldstein, for Piano, Four Hands
N 574; HH, iii. 152.

Composed 1791–2. Facs. from the autograph in *NBA*, vii (i), frontispiece.

These late skk still show uncertainty as to the correct position of the barlines. It appears that B was ready to tinker with Waldstein's theme (see 100ᵛ 1/11).

p. 87 B returned to f. 100ᵛ with a darker pen at 2/1–2, 2 + 3 + 4/6, 4/1–2, 4/5, 5 + 6 + 7/4*f*. 100ᵛ 10/8 a cross, or a cancelled semiquaver beam?

WoO 71 Variations on a Russian Dance from Wranitzky's *Das Waldmädchen*, for Piano

Publ. Apr. 1797. Wranitzky's ballet had opened in Vienna in Sept. 1796.

WoO 78 Variations on 'God save the King', for Piano

The 'God save the King' variations publ. in 1804 (WoO 78) are in C, and do not resemble this G-major sk, which may refer to an earlier version or an improvisation. See ThR, ii. 456.

Knieschieber or *Knieheber*: knee slide or lever, damping device on pianos of the time: see also the Lamentations skk, f. 96ʳ.

WoO 88 Cantata for the Elevation of Leopold II

Composed Oct. 1790. Perhaps the earliest preserved sk for a known B composition.

pp. 90–1 the continuity of these skk is not always certain. The semibreves at the beginning would accommodate the exclamation 'Germania'.

WoO 90 'Mit Mädeln sich vertragen', Aria for Bass

Assumed to have been written *c.* 1790 for the Bonn singer Joseph Lux. Facs. of a page from the autograph in *Composers' Autographs* [*Musikerhandschriften*], i, ed. W. Gerstenberg, pl. 130.

p. 90 130ᵛ 10 the intent of the referral marks ('N1') is not clear. Perhaps 10/5–7 were to have followed 10/16.

WoO 92 'Primo amore', Rondo for Soprano
Publ. in *GA*, xxv. 216–37.

Preserved only in a copyist's MS., and hitherto assumed to have been written under Salieri, *c.* 1795–1800 (see KH). But the skk, added to Bonn sheets, are in an earlier hand, and the copy is on Bonn paper (Berlin Art. 167: information kindly provided by Mr. Douglas Johnson). This ambitious aria, then, was written in Bonn, and with a German text in mind (the Italian is a translation, as indeed appears from internal literary evidence). Italian text of the line sketched: 'Ma se il dardo trapuntava gl'ambi cuori degli amanti'.

WoO 109 Trinklied ('Erhebt das Glas')

Publ. in *GA*, xxv. 267–8 (the title 'Trinklied [beim Abschied zu singen]' is not B's). Facs. of f. 107ᵛ in And., i, opp. p. 32.

Unsigned, but accepted as authentic since Thayer's *Verzeichnis*, 1865 (yet Schiedermair, p. 149, calls it 'Abschrift' rather than 'Autograph'). It was apparently Schiedermair who assigned the generally accepted date '*c.* 1787', but the writing resembles that of other MSS. dated *c.* 1790.

Staccato marks, dynamics, and many slurs were added later.

WoO 117 Der Freie Mann ('Wer ist ein freier Mann?') (Hess 146)

Early version (f. 61ʳ: Hess 146) publ. by Hess in *GA Supplement*, v. 41 (see also TR on p. 89); later version (f. 62ʳ) publ. in *GA*, xxiii. 108–9. N 561 (TR 153ᵛ 1*f*).

The poem was publ. late in 1791 (see KH) and the early version was written in Bonn, during the next year, though Hess dates it '1794 or 1795'. The later version, which differs only slightly, does seem to have been written *c*. 1795. F. 153 shows that in Bonn B also considered an entirely different setting of the poem.

p. 93 61ʳ the early version was itself corrected with a thin pen, and a new ritornello was written out. See Hess, ibid. 89.

p. 94 62ʳ 1 the heading 'No 4' refers to the position the song was to have occupied in a set B planned, but failed, to publish in 1803 (see KH 122). 62ʳ 6/5 and 9/4 B has scratched out ties and inked over the staff lines; something was also scratched out at 7 + 8 + 9/1.

Other skk: B 28 f. 36 (TR in N 562).

WoO 118 Seufzer eines Ungeliebten und Gegenliebe ('Hast du nicht Liebe zugemessen')

This unusual song, combining two separate poems by Bürger, and adumbrating the famous melody of the Choral Fantasy and the Ninth Symphony, occupied B for several years. He never published it. Skk appear on (1) f. 116, overleaf from skk for Op. 1 No. 2, publ. 1795 (2) GdMf 35 (S. 264; TR in N 536), with skk for Op. 46, 1795, and (3) B 28 f. 39 (TR in N 535), a page originally from a score of the aria 'Soll ein Schuh nicht drücken', WoO 91, which was probably written in 1796–7. (The aria is sketched on B 28 ff. 7–8 after skk for Op. 10 No. 1, 1796–8, and again after skk for the Variations on 'Là ci darem la mano', WoO 28, which were played in Dec. 1797; see N 29–31.)

The recitative with which the song begins in its final version did not figure in the earliest plan.

p. 95 116ʳ 11–13 some sums in pencil.

WoO 119 'O care selve'

Publ. in *GA*, xxv. 263–4, on the basis of another, very similar autograph, Berlin Art. 153. KH's discussion is corrected in Hess, p. 56, where the variants in the London autograph are listed. Dated by N at the end of 1794, since the Berlin autograph comes with contrapuntal studies (*B's Studien*, pp. 202, 226). A three-part canon without words on a similar melody appears in *GA Supplement*, v. 78 (Hess 247; cf. Op. 52 No. 3).

284

Red ink was used for the song text, the words 'Allegretto' and 'Coro', and the slurs in the voice line (only).

WoO 126 Opferlied ('Die Flamme lodert') (Hess 145)

Nottebohm, *Beethoveniana*, p. 51 (TR 68ᵛ 7 and 9–11, 15/1*f*). The skk refer to the early version of the song (Hess 145), publ. by Hess in *GA Supplement*, v. 15, from the autograph Berlin Gr. 8. K. Herbst, who discussed the various settings in *Neues B-Jahrbuch*, v (1933), 137–53, objected to N's date of 1794, but he did not understand that the skk appear on a bifolium with skk for Op. 1 No. 2, 1794–5. To be sure, they may have been added later. For skk for the final version, publ. in 1808, see N 478 and Nottebohm, *Ein Skizzenbuch von B*, p. 10.

p. 97 the cancelled passages on f. 68ᵛ 7 and 9 can be read only very tentatively.

Allemandes and Contredanses

The numerous dances and groups of dances sketched throughout the miscellany generally appear to have served B as abstract exercises, rather than studies for specific works. The case seems different with f. 124, a late Bonn sheet originally used for an orchestral part (see p. 125) and then filled up with some thirty allemandes and contredanses, mostly in the key of F major. References to a 'coda' point to some sort of dance set or ballet. Only one dance (124ᵛ, 8 + 9/1*f*) was reused in Vienna, for WoO 13, No. 10.

p. 99 124ᵛ 4–6 the skk on these staffs are oddly scrambled, but the sense seems clear. 9/13 it is not clear whether the '4 mal' refers to the motif (reconstructed according to 9/5) or to the semiquaver figure repeated.

Cadenza in G for Piano

Not in KH, Hess, or *NBA*, vii (vii), but mentioned by Hess in *GA Supplement*, iii. 76.

Essentially complete; written neatly on empty staffs within the autograph of the Romance in E minor (1786–7?), in a somewhat later hand. Conceivably for an outer movement of the lost work in which the Romance formed the slow movement. The marchlike theme recalls the Bonn Violin Concerto in C, Hess 10: see especially bar 80*f*.

Canon 'Meine Herren'

On a bifolium with skk for Op. 6, publ. Oct. 1797. Material from this unfinished canon was used for the canon 'Herr Graf', Hess 276 (*GA Supplement*, v. 78), which is also said to date from *c*. 1797. In Hess 276 the voices enter at 8-bar intervals.

The 'Fischtrüherl', 'Zum weissen Schwan', and 'Zu den drei Hacken' were inns that B is known to have frequented (*Neues B-Jahrbuch*, i [1924], 128–41). The 'Ochs' and the Swan are mentioned in a letter of 1798 (And. 30). The 'brothers a :' could have been the Artarias.

Canon in A

Followed by skk for Op. 8, publ. Oct. 1797.

Composition (cantata?) in B♭

Overleaf from skk for WoO 67, 1791–2. The remark about instrumentation at the bottom of f. 100ʳ may or may not refer to this piece.

Also sketched on B 28 f. 1, where the direction 'in demselbigen tempo' shows that the sections in 4/4 and 3/4 time belong to the same piece, and where a fragmentary text under the 3/4 section shows this to be a vocal work, perhaps a cantata. Part of the 3/4 section appears in score (four vocal parts and piano, with no words) in GdMf 66 [S. 296], overleaf from the song 'Klage', WoO 113; Schmidt describes it as a 'Vierstimmiger Chorsatz (B-dur) mit Klavier'.

p. 103 100ʳ 3 + 4/3 the first bars are hard to read with confidence. The words 'Gute Zeiten' may be part of the text—or a reference to strong beats. 15/5 Dr. Weise reads 'bliebemir' or 'bliebenur'.

Composition (bagatelle?) in C for Piano

Publ. by J. Werner, *The B Sketchbooks*, vi. 12–15, as a 'Study in C'. A continuation appears on GdMf 31 (S. 260: facs. in B. Bartels, *Beethoven*, 1927). As this sheet also includes a draft of the Sonata in F minor, Op. 2 No. 1 (TR in N 564–6), the C-major composition may refer to the trio of Op. 2 No. 3, as Werner suggests. However, the musical similarity is slight. 1793–5 (see note to ff. 140–1).

Composition (rondo?) in C for Piano

c. 1795 (see note to ff. 40–1). The first sk (40ᵛ) has an inscription indicating that triplets may follow. Then on 41ᵛ there is a passage in the same key and time-signature featuring triplets, and at the end of this, sketching for the original idea is resumed—in a different pen, to be sure, but on the same line (41ᵛ 3 + 4/7). It seems likely that the triplet passage was intended as a rondo episode.

p. 106 41ᵛ 5/2 the D♯ and the 'h dur' indication appear to propose a different (but equally abrupt) modulation at this point.

Composition (rondo?) in D for Piano

Publ. with wrong information by J. Werner, *The B Sketchbooks*, v. 1–2.

c. 1795 (see note to f. 53). Possibly for a concerto—if the inscription on f. 53ᵛ 7 belongs with the piece—though the style does not seem to be characteristic of that genre.

p. 107 53ᵛ 15 + 16 the inscription may refer to a rondo episode, or indicate that B meant to transpose the whole piece into E♭ (cf. the Symphony Slow Movement in E, p. 176).

Composition in D for Orchestra

Sh 524 (TR 64ʳ 13/1*f* and 9*f*), 650 (TR 114ʳ 4/7*f*, which Sh referred to Op. 20); Sh did not relate the two skk.

Sketched in 1795(?) together with Op. 14 No. 1; Sh noted a similarity to the allegretto of that sonata (cf. especially the sk on 122ʳ 6, p. 30). In spite of the reference on 115ᵛ 4/10*f* to solo and tutti, the work does not seem on stylistic grounds to be a concerto. It is possible that other orchestral fragments on 64ʳ were meant for other movements of this work.

Composition (fantasia?) in D major/minor for Piano

Sh 590–1 (TR 91ᵛ 1/1, 92ʳ 7 + 8/5*f*, 11 + 12/8*f*), 649–50 (TR 90ʳ 9 + 10/14*f*, 13 + 14/11*f*, 1 + 2/1*f*, 3 + 4/8*f*); first allegro TR in J. Schmidt-Görg, 'Ein unbekanntes Klavierstück von B', *Festschrift Hermann J. Abs*, Cologne, 1961, pp. 153–63.

Presumably the folios in question (90–5) went with 89, which is of the same paper-type (16p) and bears a fragment of an early score of Op. 19, 1795.

Ff. 90–5 transmit three long drafts or rough autographs in piano score: *A*, a scherzo-like movement in D major with a short, thematically related *alternativo* in D minor (90ʳ–91ʳ); *B*, an andante in G major (91ᵛ–92ʳ); and *C*, an extended development of the D-minor *alternativo* with new themes, ending with the word 'Fine' (92ᵛ–95ʳ). These drafts appear to map out complete movements; there are no manifest breaks in continuity, although with *C* in particular some bars are not filled in, and some of B's cuts and revisions are doubtful. F. 95ᵛ and the end of 95ʳ contain skk for *A* and *C*, most of which can be referred to specific points in the drafts.

The plain implication of the MS., with its three directly consecutive drafts, is of a cyclic composition in three movements with transitions, the outer movements using themes in common. A work of this form would not be outside the range of B's art at this period, but it would certainly be very unusual, and one naturally seeks another explanation of the material, e.g. draft *B* could be a separate piece and *C* could expand, revise, or supersede *A*. However, the more closely the 'revision' is examined the harder it is to understand, and for that matter the andante seems unlike a normal concerto or sonata slow movement. The editor adduces the following points in support of the cyclic hypothesis: (1) draft *A* shows far greater amplitude of form than does any *B* scherzo in the normal position, i.e. third or second movement; on the other hand, it makes a certain sense as the beginning of a larger piece; (2) *A* closes with the chord F♯ A C♮ (note also the cancelled C♮ just prior to the *alternativo*, p. 110) after a quiet passage well calculated to run into a slow movement in the subdominant, G major; (3) *B* closes on a tonic chord with the fifth in the top voice, a somewhat unusual detail which again may suggest transition to another movement; (4) the curious transition passage on f. 92ᵛ 1-4 (p. 119) can be understood as a 'dramatic' return from something new to old material; (5) the unprecedented development of first-movement material (the D-minor *alternativo*) as the finale may be thought to compensate for the dwarfing of this *alternativo* in the first movement by the greatly expanded *da capo*; (6) if *C* was meant to supersede *A*, skk for *A* (see especially 95ᵛ 9 + 10/13*f*, p. 113) would not follow skk for *C* on 95ᵛ. Sh took the andante to be a separate piece 'possibly for pianoforte alone', and saw the origins of Op. 5 No. 2 in the scherzo drafts, which he said were 'apparently [?] for pianoforte and some stringed instrument'. Cf. also the finale of Op. 12 No. 1.

It is striking that after proceeding so far with the piece, B went no further; he may have come to regard it as too bold, or too tendentious, for him to publish. Had he done so, he might have called it 'Fantasia' or 'Sonata quasi una fantasia'. Perhaps it is an effort to record a successful improvisation: cf. the discussion of the Rondo a Capriccio, Op. 129, by Erich Hertzmann, *Musical Quarterly*, xxxii (1946), 171-95.

At some point after writing the drafts, B returned and made a number of corrections and additions in another ink. It has not proved possible to specify all of these in the transcription.

p. 110 the first allegro is almost fully completed.

p. 112 90ᵛ 5 + 6/8*f* in this passage B systematically cancelled the last quaver of the bar by writing a quaver rest over it. For another revision, he turned to f. 95ᵛ—presumably the back of the gathering. 9/4 evidently the '8' mark does not hold in the repetition. This passage appears to have been filled in later. 14/15-18 or 17-18 may be alternatives to the staff above.

p. 113 91ʳ 6/9-10 originally a step higher, and inked over by B?

p. 116 in the andante, it appears that the left hand has been filled in only when it contains something characteristic. Unfortunately the corrections in the middle of f. 92ʳ (p. 118) are just short of clarity, but the general plan is not in doubt. 91ᵛ 5/1-2 when B cancelled these bars, he substituted 3/8-9 in the margin, changing the triplets to regular semiquavers.

286

p. 118 92ʳ 5/*end* and 11/2 the upbeat B♭ with quaver rest were substituted later for the crotchet rest.

p. 119 the second allegro is indicated much less fully than the earlier movements, with the left hand only occasionally noted, and with some whole stretches of bars left blank. The consistent use of piano score shows, however, that B continued to regard this MS. as some sort of 'working autograph', not as a mere sk. The continuity of the opening transitional passage is perhaps doubtful, as is also the interpretation of the referral marks on 94ᵛ and 95ʳ (pp. 123-4); possibly there are other cuts or breaks in continuity. Nevertheless the movement can be read as fully continuous in the MS. 92ᵛ 13 it is curious that this thematic idea does not recur later in the piece (but cf. 'N 100', p. 120).

p. 123 94ᵛ 3/14 it is suggested that B first thought to replace the cancelled passage with the one at 'N 100' on p. 120 (up to the fermata at 93ᵛ, 9/15, p. 121?), and then later added 'oder besser N 30', shortening the insert. The 'N 30' at 7/8 marks the end of the insert. Cf. also the variant at 95ᵛ 11 + 12/8*f*, p. 125. 7 + 8/8*f* in the following passage and its variant, the accidentals are uncertain. 7/16 apparently B rewrote this section several times: 7/16-18; 8/16-10/4, with the end corrected on 7/19-9/4; 95ʳ/11 + 12*f*; and probably also 95ᵛ 11 + 12/8*f* (see p. 125).

p. 124 94ᵛ 11 + 12/6-22 filled in later, at greater length than was originally envisaged. 13/8-10 a variant for a passage on f. 94ʳ was crammed into this space; see p. 122. 11/22 and 95ʳ 1/11 perhaps cuts were to be considered between the pairs of 'N 2' and '×' marks.

Another sk, for the passage on f. 91ʳ 3 + 4/10*f* (p. 113): B 28 f. 15.

Composition in G for Orchestra: Oboe Part

B's hand, from a lost B work or possibly the work of another composer. Written in Bonn.

Concerto in F for Oboe, Hess 12: Slow Movement

This work is lost, since at least 1865, when Thayer said it had once been in the possession of Artaria (*Verzeichnis*, No. 281). But fortunately *incipits* are preserved of all three movements (Beethovenhaus 135: ᴛʀ in ThF 126).

Probably written in Bonn, and rewritten in Vienna in 1793. In Nov. 1793 Haydn sent the concerto with four other works to the Elector at Bonn as evidence of B's progress as a student during his first year in Vienna—this in support of B's petition for a continuation of his subsidy. Bonn replied that most of this music, including the concerto, had already been completed and played before B's departure in Nov. 1792 (ThF 144-6, citing F. Reinöhl in *Neues B-Jahrbuch*, vi [1935], 36-47). If B revised the material in Vienna, with or without Haydn's prompting, this would account for the misunderstanding. It is also possible that B misled Haydn about the date of the pieces.

The concerto is sketched on typical Viennese paper (type 16f) used for material dated as late as 1796, and also used for the autograph of the Rondino for Wind Instruments, WoO 25 (facs. in Unger, *Bs Handschrift*, Tafel VI). This work is assumed to have been written as *Tafelmusik* in Bonn, but it could also have been revised and/or copied in Vienna.

Two fairly clear drafts show the beginning and end of the concerto slow movement. Most of the remaining skk refer to the passage preceding the trill, though they are very confused and the meaning of the various '1' and '4' signs is not always clear. On this page B entered his corrections above the original version, rather than below, as usual.

p. 126 150ᵛ 3/6 B's correction is less clear than the original.

Concerto in A for Piano: Adagio in D

Sh 333-4 (TR almost in full; Sh's most substantial transcription).

To judge from the handwriting, a work from late in the Bonn period, *c.* 1790 —certainly not as early as 1784, suggested in HH, iii. 8. The page was originally prepared for a full piano concerto score, but prepared erroneously, the strings marked ♭, the winds ♯♯. Cf. the Lamentations skk, f. 96ʳ.

This full-scale draft for a piano concerto adagio may be compared with that of the adagio in D planned for Op. 19, pp. 48-9.

p. 127 154ᵛ 1/2-4 possibly semibreve rests in these bars. 3/1-2 the 'N 1' seems to refer these bars to 1/4, but it is not clear how.

Duo in E♭ for Violin and Violoncello

Not in KH or Hess; Sh 589 (TR 130ʳ 1/1*f*).

The first half of a binary andantino, written in Bonn, possibly for B's friends A. and B. Romberg, violinist and cellist. Skk for WoO 90 (*c.* 1790) were added overleaf.

Fugue in C for Keyboard, Hess 64

Sh 651 (TR 158ʳ 1/1*f*); publ. by A. E. F. Dickinson in *Musical Times*, xcvi (1955), 76-9 (see also p. 320) and by Hess in *GA Supplement*, ix. 15-16. Questionable readings discussed by Hess, ibid. 142; see also J. V. Cockshoot, *The Fugue in B's Piano Music*, which includes a facs. of the autograph as frontispiece. Presumably written in early 1795, at the end of B's period of study with Albrechtsberger. For the inscription, Dr. Weise suggests as a possible interpretation 'but here everything can be done as at × etc.'; but there is no × to be found. The title may be 'Fuga S'.

Lamentations of Jeremiah

See Joseph Schmidt-Görg, 'Ein neuer Fund in den Skizzenbüchern Bs: die Lamentationen des Propheten Jeremias', *B-Jahrbuch*, iii (1959), 107-10, which includes between pp. 110 and 111 a complete 'diplomatic' TR of f. 96ʳ. Prof. Schmidt-Görg's findings may be summarized as follows. Wegeler tells a story about B's days as assistant organist of the Electoral Chapel at Bonn, when he had to accompany the tedious Lamentations during Holy Week. B asked a singer whether he might try to throw him out with unusual harmonizations of the chant, and after obtaining permission, succeeded only too well (ThF 81-2). The relation of f. 96 to this incident appears not only from the eccentric harmonizations of the Lamentations chant, but also from B's reference (staffs 9-10) to two Bonn Chapel singers: not Heller, the singer named in the anecdote, but Simonetti and Delombre. (B even writes 'Verwechslung'—confusion—at staff 4.) Since Simonetti came to Bonn in 1790, the anecdote and the sheet can be dated between Lent 1790 and 1792 (not earlier, as Thayer believed). Wegeler's assertion that a piano was used, as was traditional during Lent, is confirmed by the word 'Knie' at staff 12 (cf. the note to WoO 78); knee levers were attached to pianos of the time, not organs. It is to be noted also that the prank was not *extempore*.

F. 96 was damaged and clumsily mended with music paper. The letters f, o, Cla, f, and C at the left show that the sheet was originally intended for a score. Cf. the Concerto in A, f. 154.

'Diplomatic' transcription, or something like it, has been used for the main part of the page, a remarkable grid in which the chant is aligned with 9 or 10 complete or partial harmonizations with figured bass. Only a few of the figures are illegible or seemingly incorrect, though some of the progressions are certainly extreme. In addition, one can distinguish on the crowded page several other partial basses for the chant and skk for about a dozen more complex settings.

The cantus firmus as set by B differs slightly from the version given by Schindler (see *B as I Knew Him*, ed. D. MacArdle, p. 41). The last three bars accommodate the Hebrew acrostic letters.

Minuet in F for Orchestra

c. 1795 (see note to f. 99).

Quartet(?) in G for Wind Instruments and Piano

The argument for 'reconstructing' this piece runs as follows. The bifolium ff. 84-5 is devoted almost entirely to skk and drafts for two movements in the same key, G major: a large-scale movement in 4/4, of which the entire sonata-form exposition is drafted clearly, and a set of variations on 'Ah, vous dirai-je, maman' in 2/4. In both movements some stylistic features suggest

287

the participation of piano while other features (e.g. a number of high Gs) indicate other instruments—wind instruments, according to inscriptions in both movements ('fl fagotto', f. 85ʳ 3, 'Ho[he] I[nstrumente] fag', 84ᵛ 3). It would be a great coincidence if the two movements did not belong together. The 4/4 movement could not be a concerto; a chamber work for wind instruments and piano is indicated, possibly the 'quartett in g mit flauto oboe fagott' mentioned on f. 45ᵛ. Variations for piano and winds on a borrowed tune would hardly have been planned as an independent piece, but might have been planned as the finale of a larger work: cf. Op. 11. Then the few bars in C major on 85ʳ 7 + 8, which are pianistic, once again, and evidently slow, most likely refer to an interior movement.

The skk bring to mind the variation finale of the Piano Concerto in G, K. 453, by Mozart, whose piano variations on 'Ah, vous dirai-je, maman' had been publ. in 1785. Cf. Mozart's var. 5 with 84ᵛ 3/12f. B too is known to have improvised on this tune (ThF 207).

As to the date, similar paper to the bifolium in question was used in 1796 (f. 73 and the autograph of WoO 43b: see Vol. I, p. xxviii). F. 45, which mentions the quartet, dates from 1795.

p. 134 84ʳ 3/15–16 the melodic form of these and similar bars is uncertain; B has superimposed a crotchet upon the rest on beat 3. 6–8 the zigzag course indicated by the numerals is confused, but seems to be clarified by the next draft, 85ᵛ 7/7f.

p. 135 85ʳ 1f and 3f probably also for the '2ter theil' (see 2/5), or perhaps the coda, in view of the tonality of the skk. 2/5 B writes '2tel', a confusion of spelling with 'theil'(?).

p. 136 84ᵛ 3/17 there is doubtless something missing at 'N 3000', which must refer to a lost page. Possibly the following semiquavers belong to the main draft.

Romance in E minor for Flute, Bassoon, Piano, and Orchestra, Hess 13

Not listed in KH, though noted by N (p. 70) and Sh (p. 333); publ. by Hess in (1) Breitkopf & Härtel edn. PB 3704, 1952, with critical apparatus and with additions to make a complete movement, and (2) *GA Supplement*, v. 33–43, without apparatus.

Evidently the earliest piece in the miscellany; the writing resembles that of the Piano Quartets of 1785 (facs. in Schiedermair, opp. p. 224, and elsewhere), though the crotchet rest is in a later form. (In the later additions to the Romance on f. 74ᵛ, the rest is in a still later form.) Perhaps composed in 1786–7.

Fragment of a movement from a larger piece: see the *tacet* indications (for brass) on f. 74ᵛ. An old foliation 2–7 appears on 75ʳ–80ʳ. Unsigned—as

would be expected of an interior movement—but accepted as authentic by N, Sh, ThR, Hess, and Schiedermair (in the 1st edn. of *Der junge B*; in the 2nd edn. he unaccountably removed it from the canon). Presumably written for the von Westerholt family, who included an amateur pianist, flutist, and bassoonist. B also presented them with the Trio for Flute, Bassoon, and Piano, WoO 37 (KH: 'between 1786/7 and 1790'). The handwriting and paper are similar.

'Cembalo' can mean harpsichord, and Hess believes that the last two bars of the fragment show that a two-manual instrument was in question. But note the sfp marks for the cembalo on 74ᵛ, 75ᵛ.

p. 138 the word 'Gänsewurzel' ('goose-root'? in B's hand?) is unexplained.

p. 139 in the second bar, first violin, staccato wedges are written in addition to staccato dots.

p. 142 as Hess observes, the wavy line doubtless marks the point for an abbreviated *da capo*.

Rondo in A for Violin and Piano

On a bifolium with skk for Op. 19, 1795. Since the violin sonatas Op. 12 were sketched at the same time as Op. 19 (see N 46), it may be that this rondo was intended for the Sonata in A, Op. 12 No. 2, which now has a different, faster rondo in 3/4 time as finale. Other skk in A on the same bifolium may belong to the same complex. (A fragmentary Violin Sonata in A, Hess 46, appears in *GA Supplement*, ix. 115–18; Hess questions its authenticity.)

It is interesting to see the main theme change in the course of the sketching.

Sonata Movement in C (i)

Sketched overleaf from the Sonata Movement in E♭, 1797–8.

p. 147 149ʳ 7/1 B has probably compressed two separate bars here.

Sonata Movement in C (ii)

On a bifolium with skk for the Oboe Concerto, Hess 12, 1793 (or 1792).

Other skk: B 28 f. 16(?) and 56(?).

Sonata Movement in C minor (i)

N 515 (TR 143ᵛ 2/1[?]).

Sketched together with Op. 10 No. 2, Op. 9, and 11 (1797–8). Evidently for piano, since the range never exceeds high F; possibly thought of for Op. 13.

The sk on f. 101ᵛ appears to be a brief plan for the movement as a whole, touching on the main theme, the C-major theme, an indication for a *da capo*, and the coda in an early form. Such plans are not uncommon in the sketchbooks. Of the main body of the material, on the gathering ff. 143–6, the short skk at the top of the opening 143ᵛ–144ʳ were probably written first. These were followed by the draft on 143ᵛ 5 continuing on 144ʳ 4, the draft on 144ʳ 6*f*, and the draft on 144ᵛ with its associated skk. Then possibly B returned to the original draft on 143ᵛ in order to change the triplet figuration, and, with the opening 143ᵛ–144ʳ before him, commenced the next draft in the limited space at the bottom of 144ʳ (14/8*f*). This had to continue on 145ʳ. The long draft on 145ᵛ–146ʳ, which consists largely of duplication, was the last. One would suppose that B was now ready to begin the working autograph.

In spite of all these long drafts, B's intentions with this interesting movement cannot be deduced with certainty. He was considering a sonata-rondo combination of an unorthodox kind—so unorthodox, perhaps, that he abandoned the piece even after bringing it nearly to completion. To judge from the longest and latest draft, f. 145ᵛ, the form contemplated was as follows: *exposition*—theme in C minor ending with a fermata on the dominant ('calando'), triplet material in E♭, closing theme in E♭; *da capo* of the C-minor theme(?); *second section*—triplet material starting in C minor, new theme, etc., in C major, first theme in A♭ major; *recapitulation* dwelling on G major (!) and lacking the triplet material; and another, partial *da capo* followed by a relatively long coda. Earlier drafts show efforts to begin the second section in other keys.

p. 150 144ʳ 2–3 the repetition of the scale at the beginning of these staffs is hard to understand.

p. 151 143ᵛ 9/6 presumably the theme is to return here, though no *da capo* is indicated, merely the *incipit*.

p. 153 145ᵛ 1*f* the editor takes this lengthy draft to be continuous, but the possibility should be mentioned that staffs 1–2 and/or 3–7 are separate from the rest.

p. 155 145ʳ 8/4 *läuft*: runs on. B generally writes 'aü' instead of 'äū'.

Sonata Movement in C minor (ii)

Continues (another 54 bars) on B 28 f. 20ʳ. The handwriting points to the late 1790s.

The page is certainly no sketch—it is written in piano score throughout, fully continuous, and uncorrected—though as a copy, it leaves much to be desired in neatness and completeness. The style is too elementary for a B piece of this period, or even an early sk: cf. the other sonata movements sketched in the miscellany. Most likely this is a fragment of a copy of an earlier work, by B or another composer, or a piano reduction of a work for instruments (an overture?).

Sonata Movement in E♭

A plan for three movements of this sonata appears in B 28 f. 42 ('Zur Sonate aus Es'), with skk for Op. 9, 1797–8. Perhaps for violin and piano.

Song in C (i)

N 65–6 (TR 46ᵛ 6/1*f*, which N referred to Op. 15, and 46ᵛ 1/1*f*).

The bifolium ff. 46–7 was probably first used to sketch this song; it also contains cadenza skk for Op. 19, 1795 or later.

A song with chorus, for a yearly feast or celebration, according to the inscription. The five drafts would accommodate a poem with iambic lines of 4, 3, 4, 4, 3, 3, 4, and 3 feet, followed by a refrain with the words 'Heil, Heil'. (The second line sometimes seems to be repeated.) For other instances of B sketching a song in two different metres, see Op. 52 No. 3, Song in C (iii), WoO 116.

The interpretation of the drafts and skk is not always certain. At the top and top-right of f. 46ᵛ (p. 157), the repeated 'worrying' of small ideas exemplifies a kind of sketching that is seldom seen in the miscellany, though it is familiar from later sketchbooks.

p. 157 46ᵛ 6 a very similar ritornello occurs in the song 'Selbstgespräch', WoO 114, 1792.

p. 158 46ᵛ 13 the reading 'Chor' under 'oder' is questionable; Dr. Weise suggests 'Anfa[ng]???'.

Song in C (ii)

1793–5 (see note to ff. 140–1).

Song in C (iii)

Sketched overleaf from the Sonata Movement in E♭, 1797–8.

For other instances of B sketching a song in two different metres, see Op. 52 No. 3, Song in C (i), WoO 116.

Song in E♭

1795 (see note to f. 133).

Song in G (i: 'Ich sah sie heut'')

N 575 (TR 39ʳ 14/2*f*); mentioned by H. Boettcher, *B als Liederkomponist*, App. V (dated 'um 1803'!).

c. 1795 (see note to f. 39). The little song is essentially complete.

Song in G (ii: '. . . wie Pisang war im Paradies')

Sketched on a bifolium (ff. 66 and 67) with Op. 9 and 13, 1797–8.
Pisang (also *Paradiesfeige*): plantain, banana tree.

The order of the sections of the song suggested here is not certain, but seems likely on internal evidence. The problem might be solved by reference to the poem, but the editor has not succeeded in tracing it.

p. 161 67ᵛ 6 this long draft may have some breaks in continuity.

p. 162 43ᵛ 7-8 Dr. Weise reads 'trahnen', a remarkable spelling for 'Tränen' or 'Thraenen', but she sees no other reasonable alternative.

Song in G (iii: '. . . und wessen Stimm'')

1795 (see note to f. 51).

The order of the sections of the song is speculative. The problem would doubtless be solved by reference to the poem, part of which B has written out on staffs 10-11, but the editor has not succeeded in identifying it, despite the inscription at the side, 'this is "To God", if I remember rightly'. Probably this was added much later, at a time when B was reviewing his early skk (cf. f. 100). The reading of the inscription and many words in the poem is due to Dr. Weise.

Study(?) in A♭ for Piano

c. 1795 (see note to f. 60).

The page seems to have started out as a fair copy; confusion developed as to the key signature. It is likely, but not certain, that all parts of the page belong to the same work and that this work was a piano study.

Study in B♭ for Piano, Hess 58

N 361-2 (TR 153ʳ 1 + 2/1*f*); publ. in *GA Supplement*, ix. 13-14 (incomplete and incorrect).

Overleaf from skk for WoO 117, late 1791 to 1792.

A little set of variations, designated as a study by N and Hess on account of the curious inscription 'To exercise the fist'. It does not seem to be complete.

p. 165 153ʳ 1 N and Hess read the second note of bars 1 and 5 as D.

Symphony in C

N 228-9, 'Eine unvollendete Symphonie' (TR 159ʳ 8/1*f*), 511 (TR 59ʳ 1/1*f*); Sh 591-2 (TR 159ʳ 8/1*f*, 56ᵛ 5/6, etc., 159ʳ 7/13*f*, 159ᵛ 13/5*f*); Müller-Reuter, pp. 9-10 (TR 56ᵛ 5/6*f*, 7/7*f*, 16, 57ʳ 12*f*); discussed at length by Erich Hertzmann, *Musical Quarterly*, xxxii (1946), 174-8. The inscription 'Zur Simfonie' (N 228) occurs over a sk for the allegro in B 28 f. 14(?).

On p. 229 N retracted his earlier suggestion (*B's Studien*, p. 202) that these skk of the mid 1790s refer to the First Symphony, Op. 21, of 1800. Yet there are interesting points of contact, and it seems most fruitful to view these skk as a repository of unfulfilled ideas for a large C-major symphony which were later drawn upon and transformed in the composition of Op. 21 in 1800. No actual skk for Op. 21 are known. Sh and Hertzmann also pointed out similarities to Op. 15, composed 1795-8.

N dated certain of the allegro skk in 1794-5 (see notes to ff. 126-8 and 158, 159). However, other allegro skk appear on a bifolium (B 28 ff. 13-14) with skk for Op. 5, mid 1796. The second minuet was drafted later yet, in late 1796 to 1797 (f. 59), but on B 28 f. 16 it is found with skk for the allegro. If we believe that B returned to these skk in 1800, we may also believe that he returned to them in 1796-7.

The skk for the first movement, so far from holding 'little interest' (N 228), afford the best opportunity in the miscellany to observe the extended evolution of musical ideas, from primitive beginnings to the remarkable full exposition draft on f. 159ᵛ 6*f*.

p. 166 Introduction—Allegro: Preliminary Phase ff. 127 and 128 contain a number of distinct attempts to sketch an introduction in C major leading to an allegro. The editor suggests that these skk represent B's first tentative efforts to start work on a large C-major symphony. Each of the pages in question also contains some smaller skk in C major, duple time, which may reasonably be associated with the various attempts. The fifth attempt (f. 128ᵛ 5*f*, p. 167) arrives at the definitive form of the introduction and at least one idea that recurs in the definitive allegro skk.

p. 170 Definitive Phase on f. 56ʳ 5*f* the introduction is sketched at full length, and f. 71ᵛ is the first page of a 'working autograph' of this introduction (or of the whole piece). Of the allegro skk, some are necessarily obscure, but the majority can be traced to specific parts of the movement by reference to the draft on f. 159 6*f* (pp. 172-3). It is interesting that the skk seem to refer almost exclusively to the exposition.

p. 171 56ʳ 13/13 it appears that B originally ended the draft at the double bar here, and continued only after having written the variant on the next staff.

p. 173 159ᵛ 3 this may refer to the passage 16 bars later.

p. 174 Minuet a minuet in C for orchestra (see the 'Fagotto' indication) is sketched on two separate pages bearing skk for the allegro, ff. 128ᵛ, 159ʳ; presumably it was thought of for the symphony. But on B 28 f. 16ᵛ a different minuet in C figures in what is evidently a plan for the symphony as a whole—an 'adagio' in F; the second minuet, so titled; and a 'presto' in C, 12/8 time. This second minuet, which has points of contact with that of Op. 21, is drafted almost in full on f. 59ʳ, with a new trio in A minor. (This trio recalls the trio, in D minor, of the String Quartet in D, Op. 18 No. 1, 1798, while a minuet in D major that is sketched on the same sheet recalls the minuet of this same quartet.)

Ff. 56, 57, 158, and 159 contain a number of disconnected skk in C major, 6/8 time, which look like finale material, but there is no real evidence to link them to the symphony.

Other skk, for the introduction—allegro: B 28 ff. 9 (TR in N 228), 14, 16–17; GdMf 75 (contrapuntal studies; TR in Nottebohm, *B's Studien*, p. 202); and on the autograph of the Rondo a Capriccio, Op. 129 (facs. and TR in *Musical Quarterly*, xxxii [1946], 176–7).

Symphony in C minor, Hess 298

N 567, Sh 333; publ. by F. Stein in *Sammelbände der internationalen Musikgesellschaft*, xiii (1912), 131–2.

N and Sh observed the similarity between the theme and that of the Allegro con spirito of the Piano Quartet in E♭, WoO 36, 1785, and claimed that the symphony draft must have been composed earlier, but Schiedermair reasonably rejected this assumption (p. 309). Though the paper resembles that of the Romance in E minor (1786–7?), the handwriting looks somewhat later; but Hess's date of 1791–3 is too late. Perhaps sketched in 1788–9. In any case, this lengthy and relatively neat draft in full piano score is quite uncharacteristic of B's later methods of sketching.

For another, briefer Bonn symphony draft, see f. 88ᵛ.

p. 175 the spelling 'præsto' occurs in other early MSS., e.g. f. 153. 70ʳ 3/5–6 Stein read a high B♭ for the C (over which B perhaps wrote a '4' to indicate a crotchet for the quaver first written) and added editorial naturals to all the Es. 4/12–13 the minims were perhaps originally crotchets.

Symphony Slow Movement in E

Overleaf from skk for Op. 16, performed in Apr. 1797.

The notation 'in f' must indicate a change of mind on B's part (showing incidentally that the piece was not far developed). Therefore the skk in F major and D minor, 2/4 time, on the facing page (f. 82ʳ, 'Zum andante') may well refer to this movement, when transposed.

Piano Trio in E♭: Allegretto, Hess 48

Publ. in *GA Supplement*, ix. 30–4, and (without the trio fragment and without apparatus) in *NBA*, iv (ii), 219–23. Described in HH, iii. 154 as a piece for two pianos.

Dated by Hess in 'the earliest Bonn period', but in handwriting the present MS. is similar to other pages dated *c.* 1790–2.

Presumably part of a larger work, though it seems curious for B to have written two piano trios both in E♭ (this work and WoO 38) prior to the piano trios Op. 1—which also include a work in E♭. See also Op. 44. Perhaps the present allegretto was planned in connection with WoO 38.

p. 180 129ʳ 1 + 4/19 the MS. is torn, and the *GA Supplement* supplies an extra bar. However, enough paper remains to make it seem that the torn space was blank, and the passage makes good sense without the addition.

Variations on Mozart's 'Là ci darem la mano', for Violoncello and Piano(?)

The style suggests that these variations were planned for violoncello and piano, the combination for which B wrote other sets of Mozart variations (Op. 66, WoO 46). The present skk (and possibly those other works?) date from 1796, the year of B's concerts with the cellist J. P. Duport (see note to f. 158). At the same period B wrote 'Là ci darem' variations in C major for two oboes and English horn, WoO 28.

PART 2

39–42 originally a gathering; 40–1 is still a bifolium. Paper 16f. Wms: moons/REAL between 39 and 40; bow/AΣ between 41 and 42. This gathering has no skk for identified works; the clearest basis for dating it is the sk on 40ʳ 15 + 16/4f, which is also sketched on f. 47, dated 1795 or later.

39 N 359 (TR 39ᵛ 15), 363 (TR 39ᵛ 1/3f); Sh 590 (TR 39ᵛ 9 + 10/2f, 12 + 13/4f).

p. 185 39ʳ 1 + 2f cf. the song 'An Minna', WoO 115 (1792–3).

40 N 359–60 (TR 40ʳ 6/8f, 40ᵛ 5/1f); Sh 590 (TR 40ʳ 7 + 8f).

p. 189 40ᵛ 7 + 8/5f this idea also appears on f. 97 and B 28 f. 23(?).

41 Sh 461 (TR 41ʳ 5 + 6/5f, which Sh referred to Op. 49 No. 1), 590 (TR 41ʳ 12 + 13/3f).

42 N 576 (TR 42ʳ 14/11f; see Hess 321).

43 Paper 16k. Wm: three moons, cut. 1797–8 (see Song in G [ii]).

p. 194 43ʳ 6f this sk may have been added considerably later.

44 Paper 16m. Wm: three moons, cut. 1795 (see Op. 46).

45 Paper 16f. Wm: REAL. 1795 or later (see Op. 19). N 363 (TR 45ʳ 3 + 4/3f); Sh 651.

p. 195 45ʳ 1 + 2f B's annotated copy of Handel's *Six Fugues or Voluntarys for the Organ or Harpsichord* is preserved in Berlin Aut. 46 (W. Kirkendale, *Fuge und Fugato*, p. 254); see *Musical Times*, xxxv (1894), 15.

p. 196 whether the sextet and the quartet named in the margin of f. 45ᵛ refer to the skk to the right, or to other skk on the sheet, is uncertain. See the Quartet(?) in G for Wind Instruments and Piano.

46-7 bifolium. Paper 16h. No wm. The bifolium was probably first used to sketch the Song in C (i), with other material (including cadenza skk for Op. 19, 1795 or later) added subsequently.

46 many notations on f. 46ʳ also appear on other sk pages: those referring to Op. 19 on f. 89, and those at 7 + 8/1*f*, 3, and 4*f* on B 28 f. 51 (in the keys of A, D, and E♭).

47 Sh 464 (TR 47ʳ 11 + 12*f*).

48 49 originally a bifolium. Paper 10c. Wms: crest on 48; 6(?) letters, cut, on 49. 1796-7 (see Op. 16).

48 *p. 200* both the inscription on 48ᵛ and the works sketched are too fragmentary to illuminate one another.

49 *p. 201* the inscription on 49ʳ (read by Dr. Weise) is hard to understand, but the A-major draft to the right does indeed have the aspect of a concerto ritornello.

50 Paper 16e. Wm: W or VV(?), cut. 1791-2 (see below). Sh 589 (TR 50ʳ 8 + 9, 15 + 16/7*f*, 6/5*f*, which Sh related to WoO 70).

p. 204 50ᵛ 14/3*f* a very similar notation of the sound of a watchman's horn appears on f. 100ʳ, overleaf from skk for WoO 67, 1791-2.

51-4 originally a gathering. Paper 16p. Wms: three moons on 53; PS on 52; 51 and 54 blank. 1795 (see below).

51 N 359 (TR 51ʳ 5 + 6), 361 (TR 51ᵛ 1 + 2/7).

p. 204 51ʳ 1 + 2/1*f* this notation also appears on GdMf 35 [S. 264], which has skk for Op. 46 and WoO 118, 1795 (see N 536).

p. 205 51ᵛ 5 + 6/3*f* no further emendations seem to be clearly warranted; for a 'normal' version of this strange trio, cf. f. 68ʳ 15 + 16.

52 *p. 208* 52ʳ 14/2 B's boyhood friend Dr. Franz Gerhard Wegeler came to Vienna in Oct. 1794 and remained nearly two years. See f. 86. 15/2 such figures are characteristic of B's pen trials. These are generally not transcribed in the present edition.

54 Sh 589-90 (TR 54ʳ 5 + 6/1*f*, 54ᵛ 3 + 4/5*f*).

p. 209 54ʳ 1 + 2 cf. WoO 13, the trio to Allemande No. 8.

55 Paper 16f. Wm: three moons. Paper of this type was used from 1793 to 1796.

p. 213 55ᵛ 14 + 15*f* this cadenza could have been intended for Op. 19.

56-7 bifolium. Paper 16i. Wm: GF/c, cut, on 57; 56 blank. *c.* 1786 (see below).

56 *p. 213* 56ʳ 10*f* a similar sk appears on B 28 f. 13, which (like f. 56) has skk for the unfinished Symphony in C.

pp. 213-14 some of the skk on 56ᵛ and 57ʳ˙ ᵛ were probably intended for the same works in A major, 3/4, and in C major, 6/8, though the musical evidence is decisive only with 56ᵛ 1 and 6 + 7. 56ᵛ 1 may have been written later as a prelude running directly into 56ᵛ 2 (which somewhat resembles a sk possibly intended for the adagio of Op. 8; see p. 15). The C-major skk may have been intended for the finale of the Symphony in C, though a concerto finale seems more likely on stylistic grounds.

57 see above. Inscription, 57ᵛ: 'Billet an duport. Morgen Frühe.' (Müller-Reuter, p. 9); B played with the cellist J. P. Duport in Berlin in mid 1796 (cf. Op. 5 and f. 109).

58-9 originally a bifolium. Paper 10d. Wms: three moons, cut, on 58; crown/CAF(?), cut, on 59. 1796-7 (see WoO 71).

59 Sh 464 (TR 59ᵛ 2/5*f*, which Sh related to Op. 10 No. 3). Inscriptions, 59ʳ, side: 'geschrieben und gewidmet das Con. B. C. als Andenken seines aufenthalts in P' (N 511: N suggested 'Concert Babette Ceglevich' and 'Pressburg'; B's pupil Babette Keglevich received the dedications of Op. 7, which is sketched on f. 58, and Op. 15); 59ᵛ, side: 'divers 4 bagatelles de B. inglese ländler u s w.' (N 511: perhaps a notion for the publication of some of the pieces sketched).

60 Paper 16q; perhaps originally joined to f. 62 as a bifolium, into which f. 61 (bearing the same piece as f. 62) was inserted. Wm: three moons, cut. F. 62 dates from 1795 (see WoO 119).

61 Paper 16d. Wm: unicorn/C A BACH (or RACH). Late 1791 to 1792 (see WoO 117 [Hess 146]). The sheet was folded in four, and most of the verso sketched on three quarters only.

p. 216 61ᵛ 9/13*f* a similar allemande appears on a later sheet, f. 139.

62 Paper 16q; see f. 60. Wm: shield, cut. 1795 (see WoO 119). On 62ᵛ red ink was used for the song text, the words 'Allegretto' and 'Coro', and the slurs in the voice line (only).

63 Paper 16s. Wm: eagle/CFA(?), cut. Paper of this type was used in 1797-8 (see ff. 66, 67).

p. 218 63^r 4/5*f* and 6/5*f* these skk seem to refer to typical 'second group' material, in the dominant, though the latter sk can also be read in a signature of three flats. Possibly this page preserves traces of a work in E♭ for wind instruments, including an andantino in A♭.

64-5 bifolium. Paper 18. Wm: three moons, cut, on 64; shield, cut, on 65. 1795 (see Op. 19).

66 67 Paper 16s. Wm: three moons between 66 and 67, which were therefore presumably adjacent in a gathering of four sheets. 1797-8 (see Op. 9).

66 Sh 461 (TR 66^v 1/1*f*, which Sh related to Op. 13 and Op. 37).

67 *p. 221* it is probable, but not certain, that 67^r 1 is in B minor and runs directly into 2*f*; the latter also appears on B 28 f. 44, together with skk for Op. 10 No. 3.

p. 222 possibly the skk on 6/10*f* and 13/5*f* refer to Op. 10 No. 3.

68-9 bifolium; formed part of a gathering with f. 86 (q.v.). Paper 16g. Wm: crest with stars, cut, between 86 and 69; A on 68. 1794 to early 1795 (see Op. 1).

68 N 360 (TR 68^v 5 + 6/1: N reads 'Viele Sprünge'); Sh 397 (TR 68^r 5 + 6/1*f*).

p. 223 68^r 15 + 16 cf. the 'trio' in A♭ on f. 51^v 5 + 6/3*f*.

69 Sh 396 (TR 69^v 15). The inscription presumably refers to B's lessons with Albrechtsberger.

70 Paper 16b. Wm: small crest. 1788-9? (see Symphony in C minor). Inscriptions, 70^v: 'macht zusammen 4r und 3g.' (N 567), 'dir folgen meine thränen'.

71 Paper 16o. Wm: three moons. 1795-6? (see Symphony in C). N 363 (TR 71^r 1/1*f*).

72 Paper 16i. Wm: GF/c. 1795 (see WoO 8).

73 Paper 10b. No wm. Light pencil margins to guide staff ruling. 1796 (see WoO 43a).

p. 226 the skk from 73^r 7 on might have been for more mandoline works.

74-80 originally a gathering. Paper 16a. Wms: IA VA(?) on 74-7, arms of Amsterdam on 78-80. Perhaps originally written in 1786-7 (see Romance in E minor); the additions do not look much later, except for the sk on f. 74^r.

81-2 bifolium, probably originally in a gathering with f. 83. Paper 10c. Wms: crest/WVV(?), cut, on 81; 6(?) letters, cut, on 82. 1797 (see Op. 16), but the skk for Op. 37 on f. 82 may well be later.

82 Inscription, 82^r: 'Zu den neuen Sonaten [Op. 10, 1796-8] ganze kurze Menuetten. Zu der aus dem C moll bleibt das presto weg' (N 32).

83 Paper 10c. Wm: 6(?) letters, cut. Probably originally in a gathering with ff. 81-2. 1796 (see Op. 5).

p. 227 83^v 5 + 6/1*f* possibly for the Quartet(?) in G for Wind Instruments and Piano; this is sketched on different paper which, however, happens to follow directly in the manuscript (ff. 84-5).

84-5 bifolium. Paper 8. Wms: MUSIS, cut, on 84; AMICITIAE, cut, on 85. Light pencil margins to guide the staff ruling. 1796 (see Quartet[?] in G for Wind Instruments and Piano).

86 Paper 16g. Originally in a gathering with ff. 68-9. Wm: crest with stars, between 86 and 69. 1794 to early 1795 (see Op. 1). 86^v at the left of staffs 1-10, there is a line in light red crayon. At the right, the carefully lettered words 'Wegeleriana' and 'Wegeler' are not in B's hand nor, it seems, in Wegeler's signature (of which Dr. Weise kindly supplied a copy). See f. 52.

p. 227 86^v 1 the inscription alludes to the fact that the piano keyboard at this time went up only to high F.

87 Paper 16f. Wm: REAL. 1796 (see WoO 43a).

88 Paper 15a. No wm. Oct. 1790 (see WoO 88). Facs. of 88^r in *Composers' Autographs* [*Musikerhandschriften*], i, ed. W. Gerstenberg, pl. 145. N 360 (TR 88^v 7 + 8/9).

p. 228 the curious inscription (HH, iii. 29) seems to refer to the 'Linz' Symphony, Poco adagio, bar 45*f*. Cf. f. 125.

89-95 90-5 were originally a gathering, to which f. 89 also presumably belonged; 91-2 is still a bifolium. Paper 16p. Wms: three moons on 90, 94; PS on 93; 89, 91-2, 95 blank. 1795 (see Op. 19).

89 N 360 (TR 89^v 7/4).

p. 231 89^v 11 + 12/10*f* the bass for Papageno's song is hard to understand.

96 Paper 16c. Wm: fleur de lys. 1790-2 (see Lamentations of Jeremiah). Damaged and clumsily mended with music paper. The letters f, o, Cla, and C in the left margin show that the recto was originally meant for a score; cf. f. 154. Folded into quarters, one of which on the verso contains some badly faded pencil skk. The editor has not succeeded in transcribing these.

97-8 bifolium; probably originally in a gathering with f. 99 (which was, however, torn separately). Paper 16f. Wm: bow/AΣ, cut, on 97; three moons on 98. 1795 (see Op. 19).

97 *p. 233* 97ᵛ 13 + 14 this idea also appears on f. 40 and B 28 f. 23(?).

98 Sh 525 (TR 98ᵛ 3 + 4/1f, which Sh related to Op. 1 No. 2, and 98ʳ 1/1f, which he related to Op. 8).

99 Paper 16f; probably originally in a gathering with ff. 97-8 (even though torn separately): note the omission of barlines on all three sheets. Wm: three moons, cut (and torn). 1795? (see ff. 97-8).

p. 236 99ʳ 13 there is a little red sealing wax near the middle of this staff.

100 Paper 16e. Wm: W or VV(?), cut. 1791-2 (see WoO 67). N 574 (TR 100ʳ 12/1f, 5f): this poem is from Herder's *Zerstreute Blätter*, iii, 1787; the name 'Herder' was added later (cf. the Song in G [iii]). The inscription below 100ʳ 16, 'Klawier [not 'Polonaise', as in HH, iii. 16] mit concertant Violin accompagnement von 2 oboe, 2 fagotti, 2 Corni' may or may not refer to the Composition (cantata?) in B♭ on staffs 3-8 and 15-16.

p. 238 100ʳ 10 + 11 cf. the song 'Urians Reise um die Welt', Op. 52 No. 1.

101 Paper 10d. Wm: three moons, cut. 1796-8 (see Op. 10).

102 103 Paper 12e. Wm: three moons between 102 and 103, which were therefore presumably adjacent in a gathering of four sheets. 1796-8 (see Op. 10).

102 *p. 238* 102ʳ 8 + 9/1f this D-major minuet could possibly have been planned for Op. 9 No. 2. Presumably it was not this sketched minuet, but one that had been fully completed, which prompted the inscriptions at the bottom of 102ʳ: 'der Menuet ist gut.' and then, in contradiction(?), 'nicht eher das allegro gezeigt es werde dann ein Misfallen bemerkt am Menuet' (no sooner the allegro published than a mistake will be noticed in the minuet). The inscription at the right of 102ʳ refers to the sonatas Op. 10, sketched overleaf: 'Die Menuetten zu den Sonaten inskünftige nicht länger als von höch[stens] 16 bis 24 T.—' (N 35). 8 + 9/4 the 'bis'(?) seems to be written over a high G minim.

103 *p. 239* 103ʳ 7f apparently N related this cadenza to Op. 15 (N 40).

104 105 106 originally in a gathering; 105-6 were originally a bifolium. Paper 16f. Wm: three moons/REAL between 104 and 105; bow/AZ, cut, on 106. 1796? (see Op. 65).

106 106ᵛ 11-14 written in soft red pencil or crayon, which is smeared and indistinct. Inscription at the top left corner: 'Nicht immer darf der Autor seine eigentliche Absicht bej einer schrift sagen.' (Müller-Reuter, p. 149), an early example of B's liking for sententious sayings.

107-8 bifolium. Paper 12a. Wm: H BLUM, cut, on 107; fleur de lys, cut, on 108. *c.* 1790 (see WoO 109).

109 110-11 originally in a gathering; 110-11 is still a bifolium. Paper 12d. Wm: central fleur de lys; cut segments appear at the corners of the sheets. 1796-7 (see Op. 6).

109 these cello fingerings and exercises are not in B's hand. Probably they were written out for him—on his own paper—in connection with the sonatas Op. 5, played in 1796 with the cellist J. P. Duport (cf. f. 57). The editor has not been able to ascertain whether the hand is that of Duport.

112 Paper 12e. No wm. Paper of the same type was used in 1796-8.

113 Paper 16n. Wm: three moons/REAL, cut. 1795-8 (see Op. 15).

114 115 originally a bifolium(?). Paper 16j. Wm: three moons, cut, on 115; crown, cut, on 114. 1795? (see Composition in D for Orchestra).

116 Paper 16f. Wm: bow/AZ, cut. 1794-5 (see Op. 1). Originally used to begin a fair copy of the piece in C♯ major, which has the appearance of a German keyboard piece from the early part of the century. If the word 'corrente' on 116ʳ 4 refers to the same piece, it may have been the prelude to a suite. Near the bottom of the page there are some sums in pencil.

117 Paper 10e. Wm: three moons, cut. 1796-8? (see Sonata Movement in C minor [ii]).

118 Paper 16r. Wm: three moons, cut. Paper of the same type was used in 1797-8.

119 Paper 15b. Wm: shield, bent. 1796-7 (see Op. 5). This interesting sheet, possibly obtained by B on his travels of 1796 (see note to Table II, Vol. I, p. xxvii), was first used for the minuet and trio of the 'Eyeglass' Duet, WoO 32. Presumably after this work was abandoned, B used the verso for precise, heavily written notations referring to the autograph or proof of the sonatas Op. 5, publ. Feb. 1797. The latest additions were skk for Op. 16 and the imitative study on staffs 2-4. The '×' after the sixth bar—if it does not belong to the notation below—may refer to the second section, beginning at staff 6. For a similar imitative piece, see f. 153.

120 Paper 16g. Wm: A. After 1792 (see Op. 52 No. 2); paper of the same type was used in 1794-5.

121-2 bifolium. Paper 18. Wm: three moons, cut, on 122; shield with W, cut, on 121. 1795? (see Op. 14 No. 1).

121 *p. 242* 121ʳ 3+4, etc. cf. 122ᵛ 6+7.

p. 243 121ʳ 15+16 the reference to a quartet brings to mind Wegeler's report that in 1795 B was asked to write string quartets by one of his patrons, Count Apponyi (ThF 262).

122 *p. 243* 122ᵛ 6+7 cf. the notations on 121 3+4, etc.

123 probably originally joined to f. 125 as a bifolium, into which another sheet of the same period (124) was inserted. Paper 16c. Wm: NH. N 361 (TR 123ʳ 5+6/1*f*).

124 Paper 12b. Wm: crown/shield, cut. *c.* 1790-2 (see Allemandes and Contredanses).

125 see f. 123. Paper 16c. No wm.

p. 246 125ᵛ 1 for the reference to Mozart in the inscription (HH, iii. 127), see the note to f. 88. B's 'alteration of a few places in the Mozart concerto' is so free as to be unrecognizable; staffs 1-6 do, however, appear to transmit a series of pianistic fragments that might relate to a concerto. 1/9 Dr. Weise reads '3ter', in reference to the '1' and '2' marks at the beginning of the staff, but 'oder' seems to make more immediate sense.

p. 248 125ᵛ 15+16/10 'In order to work a surprise on the listener here, the final trill must turn up directly after a few bars and with that be modulated into a rather remote key [see the interrupted cadence in the excerpt] and after that [*cut*] not be developed'. B put this idea into operation in the finale of his Piano Concerto No. 1. 15+16/12*f hinan*: an octave higher?

126 127 128 originally in a gathering, in which 126 and 128 formed a bifolium(?). Paper 16i. Wm: three moons on 126; crown/A on 128; GF/c, cut, on 127. 1795? (see Op. 1).

126 Inscription, 126ᵛ: 'HaussKnecht Abends wasser holen' (N 229). Two of the contredanses on this sheet were published in WoO 14, 1802; the other four may have been sketched for the same set.

127 N 229, 63 (TR 127ᵛ 1+2*f*, which N related to Op. 18 No. 5). The inscription at 127ᵛ 11, 'thema als Rondo Behandeln, als adagio, und fuge.—', does not appear to refer to any of the neighbouring themes. An assignment from Albrechtsberger?

p. 249 127ᵛ 6/6*f* can be construed in 2/4 time if the repeat mark is thought to be misplaced by a quaver. 127ᵛ 8 and 9 pen trials?

128 *p. 249* 128ʳ 3/1*f*, 3/4*f*, 4/9*f* these skk may refer to the Symphony in C.

129 Paper 16c. Wm: NH. *c.* 1790-2 (see Piano Trio in E♭).

130 Paper 10a. No wm. *c.* 1790 (see WoO 90).

p. 250 130ᵛ 1/1 B's cross-reference is to an 'N' with the same shield-like mark on Beethovenhaus 117 [S. 91], a sk in A major, C time, 'Allegro'.

131-4 originally a gathering; 132-3 is still a bifolium. Paper 12c. Wms: three moons on 134; FC (or G) on 131; 132 and 133 blank. 1795 (see Op. 19).

132 N 359 (TR 132ᵛ 8+9/2*f*).

p. 251 the notations on 132ʳ 1*f* and 3+4/5*f*, and on 132ᵛ 1+2/1 and 3+4/3*f* may belong to the same pieces.

133 133ʳ 10-11 pen trials?

134 *p. 254* the notations on 134ʳ 3/1 and 5+6/1 may belong together.

135-8 originally in a gathering; 136-7 is still a bifolium, and 135 and 138 probably formed another (though not from the same large sheet). Paper 16k. Wms: three moons, cut, on 135 and 136; GFA on 137; GFA, cut, on 138.

138 The inscription on 138ʳ, 'war's nicht Famös am 1ten december.', is unexplained.

p. 255 138ᵛ 11+12/1 a remarkably similar progression appears in 'La Malinconia', Op. 18 No. 6, 1799.

139 Paper 16h. No wm. Dated by N '1793 at the latest' (N 27), but paper of this type was also used in 1795 and 1797-8. N 363 (TR 139ᵛ 7+8*f*); Sh 464-5 (TR 139ʳ 11+12/6*f* and 13+14/4*f*, which Sh related to Op. 27 No. 2).

p. 255 139ʳ 9+10*f* a similar allemande appears on a Bonn sheet, f. 61.

140-1 Watermarks and chain lines line up exactly between this bifolium and the bifolium 160-1; they formed part of a single large sheet and so presumably part of the same gathering. Paper 16f. Wms: three moons/REAL between 141 and 161; bow/AZ between 140 and 160. Other sheets in this gathering were (1) B 28 ff. 47-8: a notation runs directly from 48ᵛ to 141ʳ, and (2) GdMf 31 [S. 260]: the Bagatelle in C (see p. 104) continues from 161ᵛ to GdMf 31. The original order was 48, 141, 161, 31, missing sheet, 160, 140, 47. Since B 28 f. 47 has a sk for Op. 1 No. 2 (TR in N 25), and GdMf 31 has skk for Op. 2 No. 1 (TR in N 564-6), the whole complex can be dated in 1793-5.

140 *GA Supplement*, ix. 15 (TR 140ᵛ 7 + 8/3*f*: also in Sh 651). Skk for variations on this 5-bar theme appear in GdMf 66 [S. 296], added later to the autograph of the song 'Klage', WoO 113.

141 On the recto, B may have tried to chart poetic lines or stanzas with diacritical marks. Some figures and letters are written at the bottom of the verso.

p. 259 141ʳ 5 + 6*f* 'Major No 30': on B 28 f. 48, seven notes resembling this excerpt appear as the *alternativo* to an 'andante' in G minor, 3/8 time; they are marked 'Major', 'u s w. D. C. Vide N 30'.

142 Paper 10c. Wm: crest, cut. 1796 (see Op. 5).

p. 261 142ᵛ 1–4 two slightly different versions of this obscene canon are known ('. . . Martin' and '. . . Peierl'); B's text differs slightly from each.

143–6 originally a gathering; 144–5 is still a bifolium. Paper 16r. Wms: three moons/REAL between 146 and 145; GAF between 143 and 144. Late 1797 to 1798 (see Op. 11).

147–8 bifolium. Paper 16l. Wms: three moons/REAL, cut, on 148; GFA, cut, on 147. 1795 (see Op. 19).

148 *GA Supplement*, ix. 15 (TR 148ʳ 1–4: also in Sh 651). A fair copy of exercises for Albrechtsberger, later used for skk.

149 Paper 16h. No wm. 1797–8 (see Sonata Movement in E♭).

150 151 Paper 16f. Wms: three moons/REAL between 151 and 150, which were therefore presumably adjacent in a gathering of four sheets. 150ʳ followed 151ᵛ. 1792 or 1793 (see Concerto in F for Oboe).

150 the C-major skk on 150ʳ may possibly be for the Sonata Movement in C (ii).

151 the C-major skk on 151ʳ may possibly be for the Sonata Movement in C (ii).

p. 263 151ʳ 1 + 2*f* there are puzzling features about this draft, and the editorial accidentals are tentative. 151ʳ 12/8*f*, 14/1*f* tentatively interpreted as cadential passages in the dominant of D major, perhaps for the same piece as 15 + 16.

152 Paper 16t. Wm: crown/GF, cut. 1799 (see Op. 18 No. 5). The A-major items on the verso may possibly have been early ideas for the finale of Op. 18 No. 5, though it should be noted that the finale skk on the recto are late.

296

153 Paper 12b. No wm. Late 1791 to 1792 (see WoO 117). *GA Supplement*, ix. 142 (TR 153ʳ 5/3*f*).

p. 265 153ʳ 7 + 8/5*f* apparently the notion of a C♯-minor quartet—albeit a piano quartet—goes back to Bonn.

p. 266 153ʳ 9/14*f* for a similar imitative piece, see f. 119.

154 Paper 16e. No wm. Paper of the same type was used in 1791–2. The page was originally prepared for a full piano concerto score, but prepared erroneously—the strings marked ♭, the winds ♯♯. Cf. f. 96.

p. 266 154ʳ 8/1 possibly in A major, with G♮ in the last chord.

155 156 157 originally in a gathering, in which 155 and 157 formed a bifolium(?). Paper 12d. Wm: central fleur de lys; cut segments appear at the corners of the sheets. 1796–8 (see Op. 10 No. 3).

156 the relation between the items on 156ʳ and 156ᵛ 1 + 2/1*f* is not clear.

157 *p. 269* 157ᵛ 4/1*f* the word may be 'coda'. This contredanse fragment somewhat resembles a passage in the Allegro in G for Mechanical Organ, WoO 33, 1799 (*GA Supplement*, vii. 51–2). 157ᵛ 5/9*f* possibly for Op. 10 No. 3.

158 159 originally a bifolium. Paper 16i. Wms: three moons on 158; crown/A on 159. 1795 (see Fugue in C) and 1796 (see WoO 44a).

158 Facs. of 158ʳ in J. V. Cockshoot, *The Fugue in B's Piano Music*, frontispiece. In the shield on the verso: 'ne change ou [en?] mourant'. Many of the items on this crowded folio are unclear; some may have been intended for the Symphony in C or the Variations on 'Là ci darem la mano'.

p. 270 158ᵛ 14 + 15*f* cf. the trio of the second minuet for the Symphony in C, p. 174.

160–1 bifolium: see note to ff. 140–1. Paper 16f. 1793–5.

160 Sh 590 (TR 160ᵛ 15 + 16/4*f*).

p. 271 160ᵛ 1 + 2/1*f* cf. 161ʳ 15/14*f*. 160ᵛ 3 + 4*f* towards the end of this draft B seems to have slipped into A minor, and not to have reconciled the chords in the right hand with the semiquavers below.

161 Sh 590 (TR 161ʳ 3 + 4/3*f*).

p. 274 161ʳ 15/14*f* cf. 160ᵛ 1 + 2/1*f*.

162 Paper 16t. Wm: three moons, cut. The other sheet of this paper-type (f. 152) was used in 1799. On both sheets, the abbreviation 'etc.' points to a slightly later period than that of the other miscellany sheets, and on f. 162 the term 'scherzo' appears for the only time in the miscellany. The second bar in the theme of this scherzo is uncertain.